GOD FOUND ME ON THE STREET

Henryk Krzosek

GOD FOUND ME ON THE STREET

And everything that followed

———∞⋙∞———

True story
of transformation
of a homeless alcoholic

Copyright © 2022 Henryk Krzosek

All Rights Reserved.
No part of this work may be reproduced or transmitted in any form or by any means, electronic or mechanical, including photocopying, recording, or by any information storage and retrieval system, without permission in writing from the copyright owner.

ISBN: 9798841211389

Translated and edited by Piotr Błaszczyk

Cover photo: Dariusz R. Janowski

Scripture texts in this work are taken from the *New American Bible, revised edition* © 2010, 1991, 1986, 1970 Confraternity of Christian Doctrine, Washington, D.C. and are used by permission of the copyright owner. All Rights Reserved. No part of the New American Bible may be reproduced in any form without permission in writing from the copyright owner.

Preface

> *Go home to your people and tell them*
> *what the Lord has done for you,*
> *and how he has had mercy on you.*

Mark 5:19

'You have to write a book about it', said many people who heard my story. There is no doubt that writing is both a challenge and hard work, especially to an absolutely inexperienced author. To say the least. On the one hand, I have always felt this urge to share the history of my change, because I was aware that it might help others if they knew what I had been through. On the other hand though, I was scared at the mere thought of starting to write.

Now I believe the time has come. I cannot wait any longer. Not only do my friends keep on urging me to write down my story, but – first of all – the voice in my soul which, I understand, comes from the Holy Spirit.

I pray this book will help many people find their way to God. And I wish to thank God for all He has done in my life so far and for all He continues to do.

I am very grateful to everyone I mention by name in this book. My Dear Friends, without you it would have never become a reality! Please accept this book as a sign of my gratitude to all of you for being in my life. It is you who have enabled me at various stages of my life to know the great, loving God I want to serve forever.

I also want to thank the other people I have met along the paths of my life and whom I fail to name here. You have shed much new light on my pilgrimage with God. Thank you all very much!

Chapter 1

Childhood and youth

> *The true light, which enlightens everyone, was coming into the world.*
> *He was in the world,*
> *and the world came to be through him,*
> *but the world did not know him.*
> *He came to what was his own,*
> *but his own people did not accept him.*
> *But to those who did accept him he gave power to become children of God, to those*
> *who believe in his name,*
> *who were born not by natural generation nor by human choice nor by a man's decision but of God.*

John 1:9–13

IF THIS is supposed to be the story of my life, I must begin with Szczecin, the city in north-western Poland, my home town, where I spent the first 35 years of life, including seven years in prison. Then I emigrated to Germany, only to come back in early 2006. It is not easy – being over sixty now – to recall everything from childhood. Even if I dig some moments out of the darkness of the past, the strange thing is that the memories lack the joy that should be a characteristic of the cheerful, carefree stage of human existence. Scattered episodes are all I remember from my early childhood. The only longer period of time in my memory, probably two years, is that when I stayed in the country with my maternal grandparents. I remember it well for three reasons.

Firstly, my grandfather was a harsh man, who made me eat porridge with milk, without sugar, every morning. Secondly, Uncle Janek, Mom's brother, was very good to me and took me with him wherever he went. I loved him very much. Thirdly, I broke my collarbone on the farm and my arm remained immobilized with some small pieces of wood for quite a while.

The fracture soon healed properly and my eternal holidays were over – I inevitably reached my school-entry age. To attend a school I was brought back to Szczecin, where I lived with my family in a block of flats. I remember my first school books, which I received a couple of weeks before the beginning of my education. Curious about the things I would be learning, I studied the books thoroughly, with some help from my elder sister, Krystyna.

I don't remember anything noteworthy from the first three grades of school. Maybe except that I tried hard to avoid the 'big ones', as we called older and taller classmates – much older and much taller in some cases. For some reasons, the guys were lagging with their education. It may have been an irregularity resulting from the then quite recent Second World War, whose dire outcomes were still visible in Poland's landscape and the society, even in the 1960s. Postwar massive movements of people within the country, mostly poor folks 'repatriated' (or rather deported) from the eastern parts formerly belonging to Poland (now annexed by the Soviet Union) were aimed to fill the abandoned rural areas and the cities (including Szczecin) of the 'reclaimed soil', formerly belonging to the Third Reich. The repatriates that

Chapter 1 Childhood and youth

had arrived in Szczecin were mostly peasant families, with children usually lacking basic school experience. Kids, no matter how 'big', had to make up for the gaps in compulsory education.

Really hard times at school began in the fourth grade. Out of a sudden learning became drudgery, so I started indulging in truancy, which gave me that thrill. I came to a halt in the fifth grade, where I spent three consecutive years. I was just unable to learn. Nothing they lectured was at all attainable to my mind.

The other day, the math teacher, who had spent three years on futile attempts to teach me the most basic arithmetic, apparently lost both his hope and his temper and yelled out at me across the school hallway during a break, full of kids: 'Krzosek! you will never be anything!' All I understood was that if such a great authority uttered such a grave sentence, my further attendance was a waste of time. I immediately left the building and threw my school-bag into the nearest trash barrel. My primary-level education was over. And nobody in my family even noticed that.

My father's alcoholism was a tragedy for all at home. Each of us, Mom, my two sisters and I, experienced the drama in a different way. No doubt, however, Dad's alcoholism had a great impact on all of us.

I don't know why, but whenever my father was coming back home, completely drunk, he was able to reach only the entrance door of the apartment. And when he finally got up the staircase, he would sit down resting his back against the door, fall asleep, and block the passage way. And when I was coming back home from school, I was unable to enter. Those moments were scary to me. I was too weak to draw him away from the door. The mixture of embarrassment ('The neighbors might see') and fear, all the emotions were overwhelming. So I would run down the stairs, onto the streets, away from home, only to come back much later, by the dark, still with anxiety in the heart. The thoughts 'He may still lie there' or 'Everybody must have seen him' would haunt my mind the whole evening. The neighbors, the playground friends, the school mates – there was a risk to meet anyone of them the following morning. 'Who am I in their eyes? A son of a smelly alcoholic...'

This is just a piece of my childhood story. The problems I had to face as a child were many. No peaceful days, no quiet nights. What I experienced during the day would soon turn into horrors during the night.

I was scared of the dark. When the nightmares came, I would wake up in the middle of the night, and with my open eyes I could see dreadful masks showing on the walls of the room. Distorted faces. They lived! They moved. Each of them approached me. Sometimes they were animals. I closed my eyes. I tried to fall asleep quickly, but these unwanted guests kept coming back, poisoning my imagination.

I was afraid during the day. I was afraid during the night. Did my Mom understand anything of it? Did she know it? Did she worry about me? Her efforts to earn money to keep the household meant that she had no time for the children. She worked like a dog all day long so that we would have something to eat and something to wear.

I remember a couple of visits to a psychiatrist. I went there with Mom. I was even admitted to a psychiatric hospital. I also took some pills. I don't remember my condition and the results of the therapy, but I presume something was wrong with me.

The family situation – father drowning in his addiction, Mom mired in the struggle to sustain our existence – gave me an opportunity to indulge in what you might call 'free-

Chapter 1 Childhood and youth

dom'. Without the proper care of the parents, I could do whatever I wished. I lived in my own world, full of fears and painful failures on the one hand, but filled with dreams and resolutions to change it all one day in the future on the other. The future that came has shown, though, that instead of getting better, as I had planned, all was getting worse.

A son of disobedience

> *You were dead in your transgressions and sins, in which you once lived following the age of this world, following the ruler of the power of the air, the spirit that is now at work in the sons of disobedience.*
>
> Ephesians 2:1–2

With this family background, I came across some adolescent members of the underworld, who made a big impression on the youngster that I was. I admired the courage of the young thieves and I wanted to be brave, too. At least as brave as they were. I projected that this way that if I was able to draw the attention of the boys, I would finally earn their acceptance. I'm sure I succeeded in that.

My audacious bravery would often end up at a police[1] station though. The other day I went too far, and the detention lasted a little longer: I found myself in custody charged with robbery. My buddies enjoyed freedom somewhere out there, and I remained locked up. And no matter how hard did I try to become someone in the boys' eyes, my ratings reached the bottom, simply because I wasn't quick enough or smart enough to avoid handcuffs.

---

[1] Police in communist-rule Poland was called *milicja* at that time, see footnote on page 29 for more information.

Henryk Krzosek ❧ GOD FOUND ME ON THE STREET

I was less than eighteen years old when I had to face the criminal world behind bars. I had listened to a variety of stories about the life on this side of the wall. Now I was forced to taste myself how true those legends were. I was shaved my head, the prison uniform I had to wear didn't fit my size, neither in length nor width, and – what is even worse – the shoes I got had wooden soles. My appearance attracted the eyes of the other inmates. I really wanted to go unnoticed, but these shoes made so much noise! I was afraid again. 'How will I be treated by those who already know the prison life? Will they accept me as a grypsman[2]?' I needed recognition so badly that I portrayed myself as being one of them. The others – wimps, to put it mildly – were to me unworthy of a handshake (if a grypsman shook hand with a non-grypsman, he would immediately be excluded from the grypsmen society).

I was afraid that my ridiculous and pathetic appearance made me unfit and I would not be accepted by the elite to which I aspired. Luckily, a couple of friends I had met at large were serving their sentences in the same prison and they gave account in my favor. This way I achieved what I wanted. I was somebody. I was a grypsman.

Unfortunately, the price to pay for the membership in the club was high. First of all, I had to get rid of such notions as love, truth, honesty, sensibility, interdependence, compassion, happiness. Instead I was drilled into hatred (above all against the guards and the justice), rebellion, slyness, lying, contempt against men, especially weak ones. Through all this I was building another prison within myself, and I had

---

[2] Grypsmen in the subculture of Polish jails are inmates who form the 'elite'. They passively oppose any correction, set the rules of the inmate code and use the prison slang called *grypsera*. Grypsmen never compromise with guards or justice officials.

Chapter 1 Childhood and youth

no idea that it was happening. I raised inner walls which would hold me imprisoned for many years after the service.

After nine months of investigation, trials, and my attempts to obstruct the case, the court reached the verdict. I was sentenced to two and a half years imprisonment for assault with robbery. These nine months in detention taught me the unwritten code of conduct. The rules allowed me to maintain some level of active life in the confinement of the cell and the monotony and of the prison routine. I was able to slyly avoid prison regulations so that I no longer had to be ashamed of my clothes. I knew how to get a clean and fitting uniform. Being completely sound and healthy, I was able to get myself a nutrient-rich lunch ration available only for the sick. When the others ate stinking cabbage, I could delight in a piece of meat. Again, I was somebody.

Soon after the sentence I was transferred to the penitentiary in Potulice, a small town near Bydgoszcz, located in central Poland. The skills I had acquired in the detention center helped me to quickly adjust to new situations in the 'real' jail. When I was assigned to work in a furniture factory, I was smart enough to meet my daily quota without much effort. I will spare you the details of how I attained that, it is not the point. However, there is something that must be told: prison life always involves trading on an internal, secret market. Those times when I was a prisoner, three commodities were really valued: money, cigarettes and tea. Yep, black tea. If you possessed one of the three, you were able to participate in the market. I nearly always had some hidden money and some tea. Cigarettes were allowed to be kept in the locker, not too many, though.

I yearned for freedom. At night, when my cell mates slept a 'peaceful' sleep of a prisoner, I would spend hours lying on my bunk and imaging a great, new, happy life, which was sure to come true in the near future. I had to be well prepared for the moment when the gate would open for me. My imagination worked really hard during these nights. The future I visioned in my mind was absolutely bright and cheerful. I was sure to have a great plan for my future. I would fall asleep full of hope, but all that would vanish with the sound of the morning wake-up bell. Why was that so? Who stole my hope? The project was being repeatedly wiped out of my memory every morning, everything that survived was unreal and ridiculous.

I was struggling within. A hard prison life on the one hand, and a hidden desire to be happy on the other. To love and to be loved. I was young. I had to start thinking. From some distant hazy places I received signals that I had to take care of myself. But how to do it? Who can teach me that?

I was summoned by my correcting officer. 'You must go to school', he said. I was 19 already, yet I hadn't completed my primary education. Yes, I wanted to go to school, not so much that I desired learning. I knew, though, that sooner or later I will have to graduate the compulsory primary level. If not in jail, then later after being released I will have to attend an evening class. I decided not to wait, the more that the prison school opened up new opportunities for me to contact prisoners from other blocks. This also promised more benefits (trade, you know) and brought something new to the prison monotony.

So, 'Welcome school!'. I soon discovered a growing desire to learn. The motivation began to change; it was not as much about trade now, as about the willingness to graduate, and to graduate with good grades.

The first success came when I was twenty: I graduated from primary school. This might of course make you smile, but for me it was a great achievement. What is more, I grad-

Chapter 1 Childhood and youth

uated as the best student! When I was handed the certificate, I saw the grade 'excellent' in the 'Mathematics' section. This reminded me of the teacher in my fifth grade. 'Hey, Mister!' I thought, 'you may have been correct in your calculations on the blackboard, but you were definitely wrong about me. What a blunder!'

I was released soon after graduation. Full of pride and optimism, I held in my hand a school certificate with only 'good' or 'excellent' grades on it. Not a single 'pass' grade!

The brutality of prison life belonged to the past. But what now? I kept feet on the ground. I needed a job. Then, I needed to find a girlfriend to fall in love with. And she would fall in love with me too. I would love and be loved! Oh, how much I would pay for that!

Unfortunately – I collided with the harsh reality of being a former convict. The first attempt to get a job showed me already that I had to bear the consequences of my previous conduct, and it was not easy. The high grades on the school certificate did not impress much the prospective employers. The first question I was asked where I applied was: 'Why did you graduate so late?'. All I wanted then was to run away, even without my documents. I stayed for a while though, and tried to excuse this lag with some lies. That was enough. I was kindly said goodbye.

I kept on making resolutions to do something the next day. But when the next day came, I did nothing. I was afraid to go to the job center, I was afraid to talk to people. The only group where I felt reasonably well was the gang of old buddies, as well as new ones whom met behind bars not so long ago. Only in such an environment did I feel appreciated. But again I had to pay dearly for doing what my fellows accepted. Alcohol came back and so did a life at odds with law.

What should I do? How to get out of it? Who will help me out? I couldn't count on my parents. Dad was drunk all day, Mom toiling. Sisters? Did they understand anything from what I was going through? I didn't understand anything myself! It was the first time that I attempted suicide. I took a lot of medicine, so much that the body refused to take anymore. 'This is it' I thought.

I was lying on the coach, waiting for the death. I was so proud of that I was dying and nobody was seeing it. I thought 'You all will see now, but it will be too late – I will be no more.' Whether I passed out or just fell asleep, I'm not sure. All I know is that when I came round, I was surprised to see that I hadn't died, my body was coming back to life.

I did not enjoy freedom for long. Shortly after my 'death', I got caught again. No tricks this time. I committed the same crime again, so now I was a 'repeat offender' and could not expect the justice to be merciful. And indeed they were not – five years imprisonment. When I returned to my cell after hearing this cruel sentence, I didn't know what to think. I felt like crying, but showing weakness was not allowed – they might have thought I was a wimp. I tried to show I didn't care. Outside I seemed unconcerned, within I howled in despair.

I was aware I was going to serve another five years, but this time in a high-security prison. It wasn't a youth correctional facility with somewhat relaxed regime any more. I was 22 already and, after all, I was a recidivist.

Soon I found myself in a maximum security prison in Nowogard. For the next five years I was to live among people of all sorts who had one thing in common – they were all criminals. I did not believe everyone was depraved from toe to hat, surely there were good people among them, who had entered the path of crime because of wrong decisions.

Chapter 1 Childhood and youth

One thing was certain though: all prisoners in this facility were convicted of serious deliberate crimes. Financial scams, rapes, murders, robberies, various types of perversion, thefts. Now these criminals were my new social environment from which I was supposed to learn the wisdom that would prevent me from committing a crime again. What a paradox!

As soon as I learned that there was a vocational school in the facility, I decided to use the opportunity at once. I was fed up with the criminal stories the inmates kept on telling, although I must admit, some tales were really interesting or even thrilling. I wanted to learn and I wanted to learn well. There was a goal to achieve again: get a profession that would make a new beginning possible after release. I also hoped that a graduation would allow me to apply for parole sooner. There was a chance to shorten the service, so I got to work, worked hard, and I graduated two years later, with honors. As a reward for good grades, I was handed the book entitled 'Such was the Beginning of the War', written by some Soviet-army general, a veteran of the Second World War. The title page contained an hand-written inscription with congratulations. So, there was someone who recognized me! I was so proud when I was leaving the prison after the five-year service, with a book and a vocational-school certificate in my hand.

Unfortunately, the honors I got at school never helped me to get the parole. I kept on being a rebellious grypsman, which had an influence on the decisions of the court. I applied for parole twice: after having served two-thirds of the sentence, with only fifteen months remaining, and again, three months before the end. It was on a latter occasion when I read the harsh truth about me. The court ruled that I, Henryk Krzosek, 'offered no hope for improvement'. In the eyes of the justice, the five years spent behind bars did not make me any better. Perhaps it was true then. I thought about myself in exactly the same way, although I really wanted to become a righteous man. I wanted to learn, work hard, have a family. I imagined that having my own family I would never be to my children like my father was to me. But I was full of anger, blamed everyone around for what had happened to me. I desired this or another kind of revenge, but I had no idea who to take the revenge on. A prison tattoo on my hand read: 'I was born to create hell on earth'. It soon turned out that indeed I was to create hell. For myself and those I loved.

Finally came the longed-for day. I got new civvies, which were provided for by my mother. The jacket was a bit too long and too colorful, but the other clothes were okay. At the gate, while I was still inside prison, my ID and a small amount of cash were handed over to me. And the words I will never forget: 'Until next time... you'd better not come back!'. The gate slammed shut behind me. I found myself on the other side, free. All alone, with another prison experience.

I didn't know on which to build my future, I lost my goal. I left in jail all the plans for the future. All that mattered was 'here and now'. Why look ahead? I didn't realize that all my 'here and now' decisions would have their consequences someday. I made a number of wrong decisions in my youth, which cost me seven years of imprisonment. And what was inside me after all those years of penitentiary correcting? Nobody had told me how to find a way when I was young. It wasn't until many years later that I found guidance. The Bible says: Sometimes a way seems right, but the end of it leads to death! But Jesus had his own answer for me: *'I am the way'*.

Chapter 2

Life and marriage

> *For you were called for freedom, brothers.*
> *But do not use this freedom*
> *as an opportunity for the flesh;*
> *rather, serve one another through love.*

Galatians 5:13

I FELT SO RELIEVED. My criminal past was gone. It was good to know that nobody had anything against me. It seemed to me that my life was a blank page that I could write again. Only somewhere in the court archives were the files describing my former criminal activity. I liked to think that no one would ever have a reason to get them out of there.

My first job

I came back to my home town. Full of optimism, I started building my future. The first thing, however, was to get a job. I already had a profession, I was a locksmith, so my ratings were much higher than when I had left the prison for the first time. Thanks to a recommendation of my brother-in-law, who was an employee in a welding shop, I got a job for the first time. I was so happy! I immediately started to dream and plan, 'How much will I earn? What should I do with my first paycheck?' Yet fear – a good friend of mine – never left my side.

I desperately needed to conceal my criminal past. I anticipated with anxiety that I would be fired immediately when the truth about the former convict came to light. I really cared about that job, so I did anything to keep the parts of my history secret. When at the end of the shift all went to the locker-room, my emotions grew. The jolly atmosphere of the shift-finishing time was not my share because of the fright I had to hide. It was about the prison tattoos on my forearms, which were covert and were to remain so. I wondered, how to wash my greasy hands without rolling up sleeves. I lingered to avoid the washbasin as long as it was possible. When my strange behavior started to intrigue the others, I would approach the most distant lavabo, rinse my hands briefly (with the sleeves down), and leave the room quickly. I didn't want any questions.

What gave me prominence and courage in jail – was now a curse. The practice of tattooing in prison was strictly prohibited and an incident of such would be severely punished. Every now and then I was proud to demonstrate a new picture on my skin. Along with mutilation scars, which I was able to produce myself, usually by means of a razor, the tattoos created a great impression on the inmates – I was a trustworthy man. But so was then.

Now all these marks had a new, repulsive meaning, and the mutilated skin added to my complexes. Now I new I had been fooled when I had my body tattooed! But who deceived me? Sure, I couldn't have been a man of flesh and blood. I let myself be seduced by what was trendy among young criminals. It was a system that forced a certain kind

Chapter 2 Life and marriage

of attitude and behavior. I let myself be driven, not thinking about the consequences that were about to come.

Today, with my experience, I look with horror at what is happening in the world. The widespread fashion for tattooing carries the scam that a tattoo will bring something attractive to your life. It all has slipped unnoticed from behind prison bars into the world. Young people get tattooed. Adults get tattooed. Elderly people get tattooed.

Children are getting tattooed, too! There is this trend among children to tattoo the skin with some form of a sticker, usually representing some demonic characters. Isn't that an introduction for the real stuff? I appeal to parents – do not tolerate this kind of violence against your kids! I did decide myself to have my skin branded this way, and I am ashamed of this still today. Tattoo will stigmatize the person for the whole life! Are you confident that your child will not suffer from this in the future?

I am ashamed of my tattoos and I know that the inevitable consequence of making marks on the body is a curse and shame. Where does my present confidence come from? It is grounded in the word of God, who said:

> ...*and do not tattoo yourselves. I am the Lord.*
> (Leviticus 19:28)

Elsewhere, God says:

> *See, I set before you this day a blessing and a curse: a blessing for obeying the commandments of the Lord, your God, which I give you today; a curse if you do not obey the commandments of the Lord, your God, but turn aside from the way I command you today, to go after other gods, whom you do not know.* (Deuteronomy 11:26–28)

My situation changed radically when a new employee arrived at the welding shop where I worked. To my great surprise, he boasted his criminal past! I noticed that he inspired colleagues. I joined him quickly and told him my truth. Finally I felt good. I was now able to comfortably roll up my shirt sleeves, not only while washing hands, but also at work.

My wife

The next stage of my life began when I met a girl with a pretty name, Jola. It didn't take long before my another dream came true – Jola married me.

In fact we had met before, I mean – before my five-year-long service. Actually we knew each other since childhood, as we lived in the neighboring streets, went to neighboring schools, and we would run into one another every now and then for years, without paying much attention. Up to a point.

It started when we grew up to the age when boys and girls start dating. Everybody knew that Jola was my girlfriend and that I was her boyfriend. Our affection grew high. I felt so happy when I was close to her and I think she felt the same. All in all, I had somebody who cared about me. I found a sense in my life. There was someone who wanted to understand me and who accepted me the way I was. I didn't want to lose it. I wanted it to last forever. I was head over heels in love.

Sadly, the mentality I had soaked up with in prison was coming to the fore too often. 'You mustn't show what you feel!', 'Stay tough!', 'Don't say you love!', thoughts like these kept on poisoning my mind. I didn't know what to choose. On the one hand, I still had friends and my 'strongman's

Chapter 2 Life and marriage

life'; on the other, though, I was engaged with a girl who made me feel secure and accepted. I was paralyzed with indecision. If I chose my friends, it would hurt Jola and I didn't want that. If I chose the girl I loved, I would lose my friends whom I needed so much. As a result, I become a man with two faces. Whenever I was with Jola alone, I opened my heart to her. That was what I wanted indeed. When my friends showed up, I would look through her like she wasn't there. And I did it against my will!

This lasted until I got behind bars again. I had to forget Jola. All I had was the struggle to survive in the harsh prison life. For five years Jola was for me only a dream. I didn't believe she would be waiting for me so long. The moment of reunion finally came.

'What should I do? What should I say? Will she want to accept me? Will she want to talk to me at all?' Despite so many doubts and a rather chilly welcome, I was soon happy to see that she wanted to be dating with me again. I was determined to rebuild everything. My feelings for Jola revived. I just wanted to be with her. I was happy to see her returning my feelings. No matter what we had been through, what mistakes we had made – now we wanted to be together again and start all over.

'Jola, I love you!', this though dwelt in my mind all the time. Just in my mind. It was my secret. I wanted Jola to be aware of it, but I was unable to speak it out loud.

I was restrained, bound and enslaved, also when I decided to leave my buddies and stay only with Jola. Always afraid of what others might think. I thought, 'If I declare my love to Jola and she will for some reason leave me for good, the guys will think I'm a sissy', which at any cost could not be allowed to happen. So I pretended indifference, which was my way to avoid failure. This way I was hurting badly the only person I loved.

A couple of months of our clumsy attempts to build the future had passed when Jola came and announced that she was pregnant. The way I reacted was indeed both ridiculous and immature. I said, 'I don't believe you! You must bring me a medical certificate.' What did I want to achieve this way? To show how tough I was? That I was in control of the situation? Perhaps both. Anyway, the result was exactly the opposite of whatever I intended. It is only today that I understand how much I hurt the girl.

I spent a next few days thinking, 'I'm going to be a father'. And guess what, Jola did bring me the doctor's certificate. All was clear. We had to get married! The news was broken to our parents, who responded with understanding. At least that was how it looked. The parents agreed that the wedding was to take place as soon as possible, before the apparent evidence of Jola's pregnancy would cause scandal to both the family and the Church.

Our first son Arkadiusz was born five months after the wedding. I was so proud that my son has this particular name. My life took on colors even before Arkadiusz was born. I was just happy. I was also excused to take a leave from the circle of mates, without losing my status, and I was finally able to commit to working on building the family. For the first time I really enjoyed a clear conscience.

I started doing things accepted by both the group of my friends and the law-abiding society. I had to face a set of completely new problems. I was not alone any more, and we needed a home. We moved into my mother-in-law's small apartment. Being a good mother, she gave us a room to live in. Despite various opinions that mothers-in-law have, Jola's Mom is a great woman, with a specific attitude to life. She is

Chapter 2 Life and marriage

tough and resolute, but has always done all what she could to help. And she helped me a lot, too.

All the upcoming problems could be reduced to this one: I didn't know how to take care of a wife and a child. And the baby was about to arrive. The love I felt to my Jola was not a remedy to everything. Love was enough during our engagement period, but did we have a real engagement? We just went out together and, out of a sudden, Jola was pregnant. I can't recall any serious conversation between Jola and I on our common future. We just cherished the moment, all what mattered was 'here and now'. Isn't happiness all about it? However, the happiness was a temporary state, did not contribute at all to our family life, which was to come soon.

We entered the marriage completely unready, without instruction you get from your parents in a normal family. The clash with the new reality was overwhelming for me. I wasn't able to understand the woman I loved. Since we loved each other, she was supposed to want exactly the same that I wanted. Something was wrong. She was working against me! 'My wife does not understand me!' As a young married man I had basically two desires: sex and good food, but she failed to satisfy either of these. 'Why is that?', I thought. 'She should feel the same as I feel!' I considered my wife as a belonging of mine. 'If she loves me, why does she spend whole evenings with her mother chatting in the kitchen? The baby is fast asleep and she should be here with me, in bed. She's avoiding me, she must be cheating on me for sure!'

Suspicions began to grow. Alone in bed, waiting for my wife, I had thousands of thoughts swirling in my mind. All this was pushing me to the limit. I couldn't get rid of obsessive ideas. I totally didn't understand my wife.

Other areas of our marriage, such as budget management and, in particular, the way of children upbringing and everything associated with it, were also failing. I wasn't able to rise to the challenge. Decisions, decisions, decisions. I was fed up with all this! 'Is this how happiness in marriage should look like?'

Our second son was born and we gave him a beautiful name, too: Remigiusz. By then, I had built my own separate world. All important decisions belonged to my wife. I lived aside. Although I was convinced that everything was going on just fine, like in a normal, average family, I kept on building an invisible wall of misunderstanding between my wife and me. I wasn't able to communicate with the woman I loved, who was, after all, the one I really wanted to spend my life with. Over time, our conversations were becoming shorter and more emotional. 'Say something', asked Jola. 'What should I say, since I knew nothing? What does she want from me?', a voice in my mind said. 'I don't want that'.

More and more often I would join my mates after the shift, with whom I began to feel safer than at home. There were no demands, no burdens, no obligations. This way I could escape the work I had to do at home.

Among friends, we always had common, funny subjects of conversation and the jolly atmosphere grounded on 'tasting' various alcoholic beverages. Of course, Jola could not accept it. As a consequence, squabbles turned into arguments, and arguments into fights. 'Why doesn't she understand me? I love her! And I love the children. I have a job. I bring money home. And that I have a few beers with my friends every now and then. What's wrong with that?'

I badly needed a way out. I couldn't tolerate my wife's voice up all the time. Whoever seeks will find. And so did I. I discovered a great hobby, listening to music. I bought

Chapter 2 Life and marriage

myself a set of high-quality Hi-Fi equipment. I started to buy records and cassettes. I recorded music from the radio. My new passion was to get as many recordings of the world hits (especially rock music) as possible. I had a goal. Jola had no reason to be angry about that. Music belongs to the cultural achievements of mankind, and a man who knows music must be an intelligent person, right? 'I got you, wife! Now keep quiet and bow before your husband's intelligence!'

Absolutely, in order to achieve all the effects of the music you listen to, you have to turn the volume knob to the maximum. So I thought and so I did. This, however, my wife could not stand. Wanting to alleviate this conflict, without giving up my new passion, I provided myself with good, large headphones that covered the whole ears. In this way I achieved two things: I could listen to music I liked and I did not hear my wife's complaints.

I had no idea that it was the way that drove me away from my wife and my kids. Time was passing by. I did my things, Jola did hers. We were a family, but instead of living together, we lived next to each other. How very apt are here the words spoken by a man heavily tested by life, *'What I feared has come upon me'* (Job 3:25).

I did not want to be to my children what my father had been to me. And yet, a woman from the neighborhood, who new me from childhood, exclaimed a really accurate opinion, seeing me drunk the other day, 'Henryk, you're the spitting image of your father!'

Emigration to Germany

> *Like a bird far from the nest*
> *so is anyone far from home.*

Proverbs 27:8

When we came to terms with the situation in our family, a new reality opened up before us – the opportunity to move to Germany. My father-in-law was a German citizen and after spending many years in Poland, he finally returned to his homeland. As soon as he had got there, without delay, he began to organize the trip for us. The problem was that at that time it was not easy to leave the country just like that. The communist regime of the then Peoples' Republic of Poland, so very different from that in the Western democracies of the 1980s, was very restrictive, often oppressive. Many Poles dreamed about emigrating to a rich, Free-World country, to live a free life, free from the soviet-imposed political system, and free from the immanent poverty offered by the 'real socialism'. The system seldom allowed its subjects to leave; however, after a number of attempts, Jola's brother managed to flee, so I believed that there was also a chance for us, too.

My imagination got agitated anew. Suddenly I saw a number of opportunities. Better quality of life. A new life. I had thought like that before, in my prison cell. Again, I was building a new future. Just leave it all on this side of the border. All the past, with all its failures and mishaps. The freedom was waiting!

Year 1985. The regime had eased their restrictions a bit, and passports became obtainable. People waited in long

Chapter 2 Life and marriage

queues outside the *milicja*[1] offices to submit an application. Jola had already filed hers and awaited the decision. We decided to split for the purpose, since it seemed impossible to escape as the whole family[2]. An opportunity came up: a tour to Italy via Germany. We decided that Jola with our elder son will use that occasion. They might have luck. The passport application for the child was accepted. We waited in suspense. The days passed slowly, but the date when the documents had been promised to be ready was approaching. Success! they received the passports in time.

There came the moment to part. The only question we asked was for how long. The family was about to split in two, so we decided. Where would it go? We hadn't thought about it in the first place. All we expected was goodness and prosperity, for us two and for our children. We had heard so much about the riches of the West that an idea of a failure seemed absurd. Deep inside my heart, though, I had a feeling of an upcoming loss; something was about to end. When the driver closed the door and the coach pulled away with my wife and the son on board, I tried hard to keep up the appearance of 'being myself'. Yet, as I watched them vanish in the distance, an overwhelming feeling of fear and sadness came to me, which really never left me throughout the years to come.

---

[1] Police organization of the then Polish People's Republic used mostly to invigilate citizens and, if needed, exert political repression in order to affirm the totalitarian rule of the communist regime. *Milicja* was also the institution authorized to issue passports.

[2] Although going abroad was not totally banned for Polish citizens, which was the case in some other Soviet-Block countries, you still needed some reason, or 'excuse', to travel abroad, such as tourism or scholarship; it was likely that the regime would not allow you to leave the country if they suspected that you were planning to defect.

Henryk Krzosek ❧ GOD FOUND ME ON THE STREET

My wife and I had decided to leave the country mainly for economic reasons. If you think only about money, you will surely lose something. And we were no exception. As it turned out, our separation was first to last seven long months, but eventually turned into a permanent breakup. During these seven long months of waiting for the permission my hope for a better life melted gradually like ice in the sun. Efforts to obtain the passport ended every time with the same sentence uttered by the regime officer, 'Your passport will be issued as soon as your wife returns from the tour.'

I knew my wife would not come back, so my future was clear: I would stay in Poland. Jola with one son in Germany and I with the other in Poland. Was this how we imagined our marriage when deciding to emigrate? Of course not. The overwhelming fear grew stronger day by day. I felt lonely and abandoned, again. I was unable to control the situation and I was losing self-control, and still I had to take care of my little son.

The younger of the two who stayed with me was not even two at that time. Thank God, my mother-in-law was at home, and she took care of Remek (short for Remigiusz). Well, I did use that and, instead of coming home immediately after work, more and more often I hanged out with the guys on the street. I was getting drunk more often, too. Alcohol made the harsh life easier. Fear was giving way to courage. I tried to avoid the home, the child, and my mother-in-law.

However, when I had to leave my friends (or they to leave me) and return home, I was becoming aware of my helplessness. There was remorse and self-condemnation. Thoughts returned saying that I was worthless. No one needed me. I didn't deserve any good, the more my wife's love. Perhaps her leaving the country had been planned by her family from the very beginning. 'So why delude yourself? Forget it all!'

Chapter 2 Life and marriage

There came the hunger for revenge. Everyone was guilty of my situation but me. 'I'll show you all!' What would I show them? What was the best way to get revenge? 'I'll do away with myself!' But how? I was too weak for that. And so the days, weeks, months went by. I was weakening day by day, falling deeper and deeper into darkness.

I had no idea what my mother-in-law was thinking about it all. I didn't know her plans and intentions, but I felt that she never gave up plans to send me over the border. The other day she entered my room with a gloomy face and said, 'Sit down and write!', then she handed me a form to fill. 'Mom, I applied for the passport so many times, all in vain...', I tried to protest. 'Fill it out, now!', said my mother-in-law, turned her back on me and left the room. Out of fear, totally in spite of myself, I visited the passport office the following day to file the application. The officer set the date of receipt of the passport.

When the date came, I went to the office again. Again I did it *for* my mother-in-law, because I didn't believe the passport was there. 'I'll walk in and walk out, with no passport!' I thought.

What a surprise! In a matter of minutes I found myself holding a brand new booklet with my photo and my personal data in it! 'Must've been a mistake.' I thought while speeding to the exit. I had to evacuate the building quickly, before someone would take the passport back from my hands.

When I found myself on the street and cooled down a bit, I began to think about what was ahead of me. 'I will pack my cases quickly and, if they don't pull me back at the border, I will soon touch the *real* freedom'. So I thought.

Seven months after my wife left for Germany, I got on the train with the knowledge that I would never come back. I left my son because I believed that my mother-in-law would find a way for him to join us soon. Some time later, the son really joined us. By then, however, there had been no 'us' anymore.

The journey took many long hours and two border checks, during which I sweated and trembled, fearing that I might be sent back home at any time. I got off at *Hauptbahnhof*, the main train station of Hamburg. This was where my new, happy life was about to begin. My wife, my son and my father-in-law were waiting on the platform. I was happy to see them, but I also had many fears. Once again I was to face a great unknown. 'What next? How will it all go? Will I stand up to this challenge? Will I be able to take responsibility for my family here in this alien country? After all, I failed when we lived in Poland. And how will it be here?', such questions kept on coming back, again and again.

We arrived at my wife's place of residence. One room, two beds, a wardrobe and a kitchen shared with other residents – all this was a bit different from what I had imagined. 'Anyway, it looks like enough to start with', I tried to convince myself. I had my wife and a son with me, and that was all that mattered.

However, a few days later questions began to haunt me, whether I really have a wife and a son. Jola had already gathered a pack of friends, who were not my friends. She spent more time with them than with me. Something was going wrong again. I felt more and more like an intruder. 'I'm not welcome here', I thought. Jola had everything under control, and I viewed myself only as an obstacle with my life wisdom. When she was leaving the room to talk to somebody she knew, who was helpful in providing information and assistance in settling in the German system, I was leaving to the shop to get myself a beer. It couldn't last forever like that, so the other day I heard, 'Get out!'

Chapter 2 Life and marriage

I wanted to soothe her anger, but as always I didn't know how. Where was I supposed to go? I didn't know anyone here except my Jola, her father and her brother. All in all, my father-in-law declared he would help me with all the formalities necessary to obtaining German citizenship, a separate apartment and unemployment benefit. In return, I had to agree to a divorce. And so it was.

I was soon transferred to a place distant from where my family lived, a house for immigrants. There the next chapter of my drama was to take place. I was accommodated in a triple room.

Although there was a friendly and joyful atmosphere, it soon turned out that my roommates had very similar problems to mine. Each of them was carrying his own drama in the heart. The main problem was separation from the family. Most of them had left their families in Poland under unclear circumstances. I had my loved ones here, on the other side of Hamburg. But I knew well that I had already lost them. They hoped their families would someday join them and that gave them strength. Day by day, I was losing mine.

My father-in-law helped me settle all formalities needed to get the right to unemployment benefit. In this way I gained a living. I entered the everyday life of a displaced person who lost what he had so far and did not know what to do with himself. The only solution that could bring some joy to this hopelessness was alcohol. Me and my roommates agreed on one thing, that is – we deserved fun. During the months of my stay in the residence for displaced persons I can count a few days without a drinking spree in the room.

The other day I pulled myself together, gained some courage, and decided to visit my wife and the son. I didn't know what to expect from this meeting and whether it would be likely to happen at all. I decided to prepare well. First of all, I made sure to be sober. I bathed and dressed as best I could. I wanted to make a good impression on Jola, show that I was worth something. Fragrant and shaved, I got on the subway. 'Maybe she'll see some value in me and change her mind.', I thought. During the journey, I was rehearsing in my mind various scenarios of our conversation. 'If only she says *yes* to a new beginning – I will do anything for her. But what if she rejects me? Will she even want to talk? If not, then what? What will I do with myself?', I speculated restlessly. Rejection would mean that nobody needed me. I was just a problem, nothing more. No future for someone for whom nobody cares. Who should care? Why should I live then? A vague hope on the one hand. On the other – a wish to die. In a moment everything was to be decided. 'I'll see my wife face to face in a moment and she will decide everything.', I thought.

When I got there, it turned out that my wife had moved somewhere else some time before. There was no way I could get her new address. I met her friends, who still lived there, but they were not helpful at all. They kept on repeating 'We don't know.' It seemed my wife's new address was secret to me. I was full of good intentions, but it was not enough. Another failure. How many failures had already been in my life? Am I doomed to a permanent failure?

I decided to visit my father-in-law. I believed that he had not changed his address and would want to help me. Since my father-in-law had also had a problem with alcohol, I was convinced that we would get along more easily. I thought I would get some information about Jola from him. I was received warmly but not very cordially. In the beginning of our conversation he told me not to ask about Jola's address, because I would not get it. He gladly talked about how

Chapter 2 Life and marriage

she was doing well. He talked about her nice two-room apartment, the furniture she bought, that she found a job, that Arek was going to school and was a good student, and that soon her mother would bring our younger son, Remek. He encouraged me to look for a flat and a job, and to somehow arrange the life. 'But don't think about returning to your wife and the children, because Jola doesn't want you anymore.'

At one point my father-in-law went out to the bathroom for a moment. As I looked around his room, my eyes stopped for a moment on the telephone table. I saw a small piece of paper lying on the phone. I came over and saw that it was my wife's phone number. The man could come back any time, and there was no way to write down the information, so I had to memorize it. We didn't talk long after he returned. He was still saying something, and at that time I was repeating these eight 'life-saving' digits in my mind. I couldn't forget them. They were like all my hope.

I had some sort of point of contact. But from the moment I got the phone number to the moment I talked to Jola some time passed, which was entirely filled with boozing. I didn't see it that way at the time, but vodka, wine, and beer were the masters of my behavior.

Then something happened that still today moves me deeply. The other day I was standing on the platform of a subway station with some buddies, waiting for a train. I was in a good, tipsy mood. When the *S-Bahn* pulled to a stop, I saw my wife, mother-in-law and a little boy get off through the door we were about to board. This went on for a while after I got on the train: 'Hi – hi.' 'How are you?' 'I'm fine.' And the train door closed in front of me with a hiss. That boy, it was my son, Remek. Our eyes met. His sad eyes, his sad face, were so meaningful. It was as if he wanted to tell me something, but I was moving away. The train left. I can't describe how much pain pierced my heart at that moment. How much despair I fell into. And that helplessness. 'My little Son, I don't want this! Why are we moving away from each other?! You don't want it either, do you? Your eyes tell me that...What am I doing?!'

At the next station, leaving my buddies behind, I almost jumped off the train. I wanted to escape. Not just from my friends, but from the whole situation I was in. To escape from the pain that was growing inside me. Until dawn, I wandered the empty streets of Hamburg. Only tears were the answer to my helplessness. In the morning, exhausted mentally and physically, I returned to my room. I lay down but could not sleep. Then I remembered that I had a gun among my clothes in my travel bag. Admittedly, it was a tear-gas pistol, but it was of a large caliber. I hoped that by some miracle the gas bullet would turn into a real one. I put it against my temple and pulled the trigger. Bang, smoke, stench, and burned skin on my temple, and I was alive. Again, a failure.

After this incident, a friend who had just gotten an apartment, and with whom I got along in various areas – including alcohol – offered me to move in with him. I accepted the offer with joy, because there was another opportunity for a change. Maybe now it would work? But soon it turned out that the desire for change and a new life was dying in the same place where it was born. In the sphere of my intentions. My friend, already having an independent apartment, decided to bring his wife from Poland. When he told me about it and told me the date of her arrival, I understood that my stay in his apartment was coming to an end. From that moment on I felt at every step that my friend wanted to get rid of me as soon as possible. I knew I had to go, but

Chapter 2 Life and marriage

I didn't know where. The day came when I decided that I would not come back to Krzysiek's apartment. The first night of my homelessness I slept in an underground garage.

The street, my new home

> *But the deed of the Lord they do not regard,*
> *the work of his hands they do not see!*
> *Therefore my people go into exile*
> *for lack of understanding,*
> *Its nobles starving,*
> *its masses parched with thirst.*
> *Therefore Sheol enlarges its throat*
> *and opens its mouth beyond measure.*
>
> Isaiah 5:12b–14a

I still had some money, because I was getting unemployment benefit all that time. But I didn't have a roof over my head anymore, so this benefit had to end. I had to drink, but I had no money to pay for it. I started to steal alcohol in stores. After a short time and more arrests by the police, I was tried for my thefts and locked up in jail for three months. Somehow, I lasted through that time without drinking. Under lock and key I even took up a job and managed to earn something. And again, just like before, when I was serving my sentence, I would lie on the bunk and arrange my life in my mind. I was not idle; with the help of the prison counselor, I gathered information about where I could go to seek help after leaving the jail. I learned about social benefit rights and how to get them. Of course, when the prison gates opened for me again, my first steps were to a liquor store. I didn't speak German well enough, and I had to deal with German officials. To boost my spirits I recharged a little. In the social office I was treated very well. Right away they found an interpreter for me, with help of which I could arrange for necessary accommodation and fill proper forms for granting the social allowance. The people at the office were so good to me. They called around to different places and found a one-room apartment for me to rent. Everything was falling into place. I got the benefit, I had a place to live. I could start a new life. But I had to pull myself together. I did well at first. I didn't stop drinking, but I cut it down drastically. After all, I had my wife's phone number. I wanted to get in touch with her. I knew I had to prepare myself well for that.

Once I decided I was ready enough, I worked up the courage to walk into a phone booth. I didn't know what I was going to say. 'What is to be, will be'. I dialed the number and after a while, for the first time in months, I heard my wife's voice again. The conversation was warm, but Jola was relentless. I shouldn't get my hopes up for a future together. She also didn't want to give me a new home address, and I couldn't think about seeing the kids, either.

After this conversation, my hope that something could still be rebuilt completely melted away. I came to the conclusion that there is no point in trying anymore. I had to accept the fact that we would never be together again. During this time, something happened that later amused me greatly. When my wife made it clear that there was no coming back for me, I wanted to prove at all costs that I loved her and I loved the children. I wanted to give them some kind of sign. Let it be the last sign in my life. I devised another suicide attempt. This time I was going to hang myself from the cable of a TV antenna. I bought a bottle of vodka. I took the pictures of my children out of the drawer and started to prepare the cable on which, with the pictures of my children in my hands, I

Chapter 2 Life and marriage

was to hang myself. The cable was a little stiff and I was having a hard time, so every now and then I would reach into the bottle. When I was done with everything and the noose was around my neck, I took one last, deeper sip. It was to be the last sip in my life. A little tired of all this, I laid down on my bed to rest a bit before the final step. I woke up the next day, with a noose around my neck, but no more desire to die! Today, when I look back on this event, I have a great laugh. I know that many of the misfortunes in my life so far have been inspired by the whispers of Satan. He was the one who gave me ideas that ended in my failures. He is the one who has given me ideas of ending up with myself. He was also the one who whispered in my ear, 'Have a drink!' Funny, but in this case, Satan was caught in his own snares. He was prompting me, 'Hang yourself!', but also, 'Drink!' In this situation of mine, one precluded the other. To hang myself I needed to work up the courage, so I needed to drink. On the other hand, I drank so much that I forgot to hang myself!

After that ridiculous suicide attempt, I gave it a rest – for a while. I decided to accept the principle: let whatever happens. After all, I had a roof over my head. The social benefit I received was not at all small – considering my modest needs. I was independent. To add something to my loneliness, I started to visit the entertainment bars in the famous borough of Hamburg called *St. Pauli*. I didn't realize at the time that soon enough the streets I was roaming from bar to bar would become my home. I met a new bar society. I was also offered a casual job. For a while my day looked like this: go to work in the morning to earn some money, and in the evening to the pub to spend it ostentatiously. I liked this life. The eyes of others were on me. This was what I had wanted since my early youth. Now I was catching wind in my sails. Just as the wind doesn't blow with the same force all the time, my ratings plummeted when I was fired from job. I wanted to stay on an even financial footing. After all, I couldn't show my friends that I had begun to fail in every way. When I received another unemployment benefit, which was supposed to cover the costs of my dwelling, I faced a dilemma: pay for the apartment or drink it with my friends. Friends seemed more valuable to me. The first month I managed to do it. The next month I received the check and did not pay the rent for the second time. I also took my chance in the third month. And here is where I miscounted. I came home late at night, wanted to unlock the door, and the key didn't fit. The lock had been replaced. This way the owner got rid of a nuisance tenant, an alcoholic who notoriously failed to pay the rent.

Without disclosing my situation to anyone, I would buy alcohol for those who allowed me to stay overnight. Somehow, I was able to get by. When the long-awaited check was about to come, I would be waiting for the postman outside the house of my former residence early in the morning. Those days the mail service would bring the check together with the mail. I succeeded! I caught the letter carrier in the street and with the money in my pocket I set out to conquer another *Kneipe*.

But I made a cardinal mistake. Shortly before I was kicked out of my apartment, the *Sozialamt* had sent me a form to fill, which I was supposed to send back if I wanted to receive my money again. In my drunken amok, however, I kept postponing this simple action 'till tomorrow', day by day. Then came that unfortunate night, when I was denied access to my apartment, and all my belongings stayed inside – including the form. As it soon turned out, failure to complete this formality sealed my tragic new beginning. How many

Chapter 2 Life and marriage

times had this already happened? I didn't know. I still had some hope, which was the next visit of the postman. Up to that point, I had spent several nights at a friend's house. But when my money supply ran out, they quickly gave up on me. 'When I get the money, they will let me in again' – I thought. Just like a month before, I was there, looking forward to receiving a new check. Suddenly I saw the postman from a distance. My heart was working at its peak speed. 'Does he have the money or not?' The man came closer, so I came out of hiding. 'Nothing for you this time, Sir.' I didn't believe him. Asked him to search through the money orders again. Nothing. A cruel reality reached me – I was left without any means of subsistence. No roof over my head. Without friends or buddies. No family. The streets became my home. How true were the words of God from the Book of Isaiah (5:14), just for me, *'Therefore Sheol enlarges its throat and opens its mouth beyond measure.'*

Chapter 3

My nighttime shelters

> *He will pass through it hard-pressed and hungry,*
> *and when hungry, shall become enraged,*
> *and curse king and gods.*
> *He will look upward,*
> *and will gaze at the earth,*
> *But will see only distress and darkness,*
> *oppressive gloom,*
> *murky, without light.*

Isaiah 8:21–22

THE BEGINNING of my new life on the streets wasn't easy, although the weather was very good. It was the high summer season. Days were hot and nights were nice and warm. I didn't have to worry about where I would sleep; the problem was where I would drink. The first few weeks I walked down the streets and across parks watching the lives of other homeless people. I wanted to join them but I knew my German was still very poor. How to break through and join this companionship? As Poles say, 'Vodka unties tongues.' Maybe this was the way, but to succeed you need to have some vodka in the first place. 'Maybe I should try and get some in a liquor store?' I thought. With this idea in mind I went to examine the neighborhood. I visited one store, then another. I watched the staff, the location of the checkout, the arrangement of the shelves and the exit routes, my brain working at its peak. Soon, after having inspected several stores, I decided that a big grocery would best suit my plans. Off we go! I entered the shop. There was nothing like a security gate, so you could easily enter, but the exit was only through the checkout. The round mirrors hanging from the ceiling here and there looked scary, yet I took my chance. I didn't know whether anyone was watching me pass by the stand packed with bottles. I reached down quickly and a bottle was right behind my trouser belt. 'Now, how to get out?' I strolled along the racks of shelves for a while, like an ordinary shopper, took courage, and swiftly left the shop. Piece of cake! My first 'acquisition'. Glad of this, I decided that I would come back here, and I did, quite often. For some time it was my favorite 'shopping' place.

Approaching my friends-to-be with such an 'argument' in hand wasn't difficult now. A moment later, I shared the bottle with a group of the other homeless. My generosity probably got appreciated, as I was offered to have a meal with them in a soup kitchen. This way I learned where I could get some food, change dirty clothes, take a shower or shave my face. My new friends showed me many places where the homeless would get help: meal sites, aid centers operated by churches, and the *Caritas*. The situation looked not that bad any more.

However, it was still on me to satisfy my two other 'basic' needs, which were a place to sleep and... alcohol supply. Perhaps the former wasn't that much of a problem at that time, because the nights were still warm, and I often fell asleep just where I got drunk. It wasn't always a night. Sometimes I took a nap on the grass or on a bench in a park, or in some yard. I even preferred a nap during the day,

Chapter 3 My nighttime shelters

because that allowed me to gather more strength for the hunting nights.

The district called *St. Pauli* is the most prominent part of Hamburg. It is known for the fact that when the other parts of the city peacefully fall asleep, life at *St. Pauli* wakes up and all kinds of entertainment continue until dawn. That is why *St. Pauli* was a good place for me in terms of the most important need of mine – thirst. The area is packed with bars, which fill with people having fun every night. Parties ran not only inside the facilities – where I was not allowed to enter – but often poured outside, into the streets, participants occupying benches or sitting on the grass in the nearby parks. The homeless were 'served' there. Among all the fine restaurants and less expensive diners, there was a very special licensed establishment, the cheapest place for the poorest clients. The sign by the entrance encouraged to drop in, saying, 'The cheapest *Knaipe* in the area! *Der Clochard*. Open all day!' Unfortunately, you still had to own some petty cash to sit there. I usually failed to meet this requirement. Anyway, even if I possessed some money, I chose the unrestricted outdoor space to relax.

When everybody in *St. Pauli* were busy having fun, coming across some alcohol leftovers was really easy. In most cases it was beer, but unfinished bottles of wine or *Schnaps* happened too. It was not a problem to me that most of it had been drunk by some other people. It was important that it was there. I liked those nighttime hunting tours. Not only could I get drunk every day, but I was also able to store something for the following day. The best were the mornings. The sun was about to rise, the pubs were empty, and the last guests on their way home were leaving their unfinished drinks wherever they could. Everything that I could miss in the darkness emerged in the morning.

Henryk Krzosek ❧ GOD FOUND ME ON THE STREET

I had to hurry, though, because the cleaning services were entering the scene as early as at dawn. The thorough street cleaning was about to begin, involving both big garbage trucks and sweeping teams equipped with trolleys, brooms and buckets. At six in the morning the big cleaning was over. The streets were all clean again, until evening. My best catches were sure to happen on Fridays and Saturdays. Of course, non-working days. During the week it was different, but it wasn't bad at all. If I had not found alcohol, I would collect bottles. It was also money. When I sold them in the morning, I had a lot of money to buy a drink. I was constantly wandering the streets.

Nearby was the *FC St. Pauli* stadium. And although at that time it was a second-league team, thousands of loyal supporters would come to watch them play. I was looking forward to a match, which was usually held every two weeks, not because I was a fan of football, but because hectoliters of beer were drunk and tons of sausages were eaten during a sports event. Around the stadium were stands offering these goodies. Afterwards, unfinished beers, uneaten sausages and leftover sandwiches were everywhere. It was a real feast for me.

When I got to know the stadium, I thought that maybe somewhere there I would find a temporary home. The whole area was fenced and all gates were closed, but I was sure to be able to climb over the fence. I arrived there in the evening. I got over the fence without a problem and after a while I was inspecting every part of the place. I was looking for some roofed space, suitable for sleeping, like a locker room for example. Commentary cabins were locked, but at the very top of the stadium, where TV-cameras would probably be installed for matches, I saw a long bench. When I came closer, I saw that it was basically a long box with a

Chapter 3 My nighttime shelters

lid. I lifted the cover up, there was nothing inside. I thought, 'Here I can store my treasures: collected bottles and stuff.' I had another thought, 'If I found a sleeping bag or something, I could also store it here too.' The idea started to shine in my mind: the nights were getting colder and colder and it would start freezing soon. I found an excellent shelter!

Collections of bulky-waste, called *Sperrmüll*, were carried out in Hamburg those days. On a previously announced date, the inhabitants of the area would take everything from their homes which was no longer needed and place it all outside, right on the sidewalk. You might have got rich on such a *Sperrmüll* day, therefore lots of scavengers were browsing the discarded things, mostly early in the morning. I learned about the nearest collection day in my neighborhood from a phone book and, when it came, I joined a group of collectors. Unlike the others, I was only interested in bedding articles. Very quickly I found a good, thick sleeping bag. Under cover of night, with the sleeping bag under my arm, I got to the stadium.

Before that time I had slept in underground garages, on cartons found near shops. The first layer of my 'bed' was concrete, the second was cardboard, and the third was me. It was neither hard nor cold. The biggest problem in my favorite garage on *St. Pauli*, which originally was an old, war-time air-raid shelter, was vermin, mice and rats. I often had to run away from this company at night.

Sometimes, a police patrol would drive me out of my 'bedroom' in the middle of the night. Being homeless in this place – as the police explained – was absolutely prohibited. But what was I supposed to do? Although it was a nasty and dangerous place, I kept coming back.

It would change now. I was very happy with my new accommodation. No longer concrete, but a wooden 'bed'.

I got used to bad conditions when in jail, as I was often punished with sleeping on a hard, mattress-free bed. I spent the first night at the stadium in my sleeping bag and, most importantly, without shoes on my feet. For the first time in many months I could sleep with my shoes off! What a relief!

I was foraging for alcohol at night, and only at night was my new accommodation accessible, so, although it was a cozy place to sleep, I could not use it very often. Anyway, I was proud to have my own corner. For a while at least.

The other night unexpected guests came, two policemen visited my 'home'. They woke me up and muttered something. With a hangover, still half asleep, I could only guess they wanted to check my identity. At that time I still had an ID, which stated that I did not have a permanent residence. The officers, seeing that the conversation with me was a waste of time, talked for a moment, made a few calls, told me to take all my belongings and go with them. We left through the gate. They gave me back my ID, warned me not to enter the stadium again, got into their police car and drove away. I was left alone on the street with the sleeping bag in my hand. I hid the sleeping bag in the bushes and went wandering the streets.

Again, for a time, I would fall asleep where I got drunk. It was getting cold, and frosty nights were more and more common. My sleeping bag, hidden in the bushes, got soaked in the rain and was useless. Under these circumstances, having no access to either the garage or the stadium, I had to invent something new. And I found a new, uncertain though dry and warm place to rest. I got on the subway, chose a seat in the rear and fell asleep. I traveled there and back. Of course I got caught for riding without a ticket, but I didn't care. Only later did it turn out how heavy were the consequences. Now, however, the most important thing for

Chapter 3 My nighttime shelters

me was that I could warm up and have a sleep, for a while at least.

One morning I woke up in a strange place. I soon realized that it was the construction site of a new hotel at *Landungsbücken* (a walking site with a nice view on the Elbe and the harbor). How I had got there, I had no idea. I must have been so drunk that I wasn't able to recall anything from the previous day. Anyway, I thought it would be a good place to stay. I decided to check it out the following night. As soon as the builders finished their work, I sneaked in and evaluated the place. I had an easy task, because not long before I found a small flashlight in the park. It was useful during my nightly tours and now it was to help me find a room at the construction site. The building under construction had many floors and many rooms. I thought the smallest room on the top floor would be the safest place to stay.

You can imagine how it is on a construction site – dust and debris everywhere. So after the first night I was all over dirty and I needed to do something about it. I brought some cartons from the garbage containers near a shop, which served well as a bed. Again I had my place.

Unfortunately, it again didn't last long. Although the construction was advanced, the hotel still had no windows or doors. The wind didn't stop. Drafts made the cold nights even colder. It was not a good place for the winter.

The winter

> *And he longed to eat his fill of the pods on which the swine fed, but nobody gave him any.*

Luke 15:16

The construction works went on. The first stages were planned to be completed before the winter. Doors and windows had been installed; however, an office container appeared by the fence, for a guard and a dog. This meant of course that I had to say goodbye to my construction site.

Fewer and fewer people visited *St. Pauli* as the cold season proceeded. There was no sense in looking for a good place in parks either. I was ashamed of going to soup kitchens in my condition. I started wandering around the garbage cans. I collected bottles. I discovered that in the trash-bins near schools you could even find packaged sandwiches. I managed somehow. Unfortunately, I still needed alcohol, which I stole from shops. Police would recognize me more and more often.

The other day I came across an interesting dumpster. Not because I could find something in it. It had other advantages. It was an office dumpster, very well maintained, located in a clean and – most importantly – warm room. Inside the garbage containers, there were big blue bags filled with shredded paper: an ideal place to sleep on winter nights. Whenever I came there, I moved the last two trash containers, spread two bags behind them and slept warm until dawn.

Although my situation seemed to improve again, it was getting harder anyway. The motivation one needs to survive was gradually diminishing. Especially when the alcohol

Chapter 3 My nighttime shelters

evaporated a little, the awareness of my position would return. At such moments I was tormented by thoughts of suicide. 'How about ending it all? How to do it effectively?' In this mood, after a failed attempt to shop-lift a bottle from a store, I was arrested. With a dire need of a drink I found myself behind bars and there was nothing I could do. I felt so powerless that I began to cry. I had enough of it all! Then the thought appeared, 'Do something to make the police shoot you.' But what should I do? Various thoughts swirled inside my head, but finally I had a good plan. I knew how to provoke a policeman to shoot me dead.

During the arrest, the detainee's documents and money are taken, but also, for security reasons, various sharp objects, shoelaces, a trouser belt and a lighter. Cigarettes are allowed. When a detained smoker wants to light a cigarette, he or she knocks on the door and after a while a guard comes with fire. I saw this as my chance. The plan was that I would ask for light, and when the policeman opens the door, I would assault him, snatch the gun from his holster and aim it straight at him. Then other policemen should definitely come with rescue and, seeing me with a pointed weapon, shoot me down. And it would be all over.

I moved on to action. First, a policeman asked through the door why I was knocking. When I replied that I wanted to smoke, he announced that he would come with fire in a moment. I was really focused. My muscles tense, like a tiger ready to attack. The cell door opened and the policeman stood there. He was about to become my victim. The policeman lit the lighter, I threw myself at him, reached for the pistol, and... three other cops knocked me down to the floor and handcuffed me. Lying face down, I only heard the clink of a key in the lock.

I have planned everything so well – and again failure. As a consolation, I could hope that after this incident of an active assault on a police officer, they would put me in prison. It was also an idea for surviving winter. And here disappointment: I was released the following day.

I could do what I wanted but I was not happy with it. The weather was not so good. Frost, then thaw, then frost again, and so on. I was forced to underground, literally – I went down to a subway station. It was warmer there, which didn't mean that it was safer. Frequent checks by police and subway guards made my life difficult. You were not allowed to be on the platform without a valid ticket, and I never had one.

I still had my ID, however. I soon learned how to make a smart use of it. Whenever I was asked for a fare-ticket, I gladly presented my ID card, which was needed by the controller to issue the fine. I got a receipt, and it allowed me to travel by train until the last hour of the day. That was great! Riding all-day on a warm train. After some time I knew all about the subway stations. I knew which were warm and which were cold and, therefore, not worth bothering. I also knew which benches were comfortable to sleep on. *Landungsbrücken* was my favorite station. It was really warm with the most comfortable seats. All you needed to do was jump upstairs, pick something from the store, and return to the warmth.

The other day I was robbed while sleeping on a platform bench. The remains of my documents were stolen. I was left with nothing. I couldn't even prove that I was me.

The winter was well underway and I felt worse and worse. I was drunk or hung over all the time. Dirty and tired. In clothes that gave no protection against the cold. Every now and then I was caught without a ticket. I had no documents,

Chapter 3 My nighttime shelters

so I was handed over to the police, who, after writing a report, let me go.

After one of these arrests, I was given a written prohibition to enter the *U-Bahn* stations. I don't know why they issued the document, since it was only in my pocket and only I knew about it. The ban did not change anything in my conduct. On the contrary, it gave me hope that the police, seeing my stubbornness, would eventually lock me up. I wanted to go to prison to survive the winter, but I was still free!

Once again I was caught stealing vodka from a store. The police were called, a short conversation took place, and I ended up in a police car and then in detention. Because I have often visited that particular police station recently, this time the police got more inquisitive about me. An interpreter was called and a long conversation was held with me. I told them my whole story – how I got to Germany, what happened to my family, why I'm homeless. I felt that they wanted to help me! And I wanted them to lock me up. When I was released, I received a referral to another police station. There I was supposed to meet people who would try to change my life. What could I expect? I thought that there was no rescue for me. I wanted to get to prison because it was warm! I asked them to arrest me. I was convinced that I had stolen enough and traveled without paying the fare that they had a good reason to lock me behind bars.

Seeing that this made no impression on the police officers, I used, as it seemed at the time, a serious argument: 'If you let me go, I will be stealing in shops again!' Then a policewoman said it would be better if I went to steal in another district of the city, because 'they have their hands full here'.

And so I did. I moved to *Altona*, another borough of Hamburg. I stole a large bottle of rum. I drank a little and, with the rest in hand, I returned to the police station which I had left not so long before. I showed the policemen what I had stolen. I said where and in which shop. I thought that with such evidence they would have to imprison me. However, after a while, accompanied by two police officers, I was led outside. Devastated, I sat on the stairs. A moment later, one of the policeman came out. All hope returned for a moment! Maybe they will lock me up now? The policeman carried my stolen bottle of rum, put it near my feet, turned on his heel and left without a word. What a fate! They didn't even want me in prison!

I had no choice. I had to break through. I started visiting soup kitchens again. At that time they were open from 2 to 6 in the evening. Four hours in a warm place – it's always something. I could take a nap while sitting at the table. Many of my street buddies used this opportunity too. It was very usual: some were eating soup, some waiting in line to take a shower, some queuing to get clean clothes, and some snoring loudly.

Many months of continuous drinking degraded my body to such a condition that I became all shaky. Everything was trembling in me. I was swollen. Sometimes it felt like that unless I quickly had a drink, my body would explode. The sobriety was the worst. When I was drunk I didn't feel hungry, so I didn't visit soup kitchens. But when I sobered, the hunger appeared. It was cold too. On the one hand, there was hunger, which I could satisfy in the soup kitchen. On the other hand, however, there were the dire symptoms of alcohol poisoning. It was horrible!

When I finally decided to come and have a meal, I was unable to hold the plate with soup in my trembling hands. Even if I managed to carry the soup to the table without spilling it all along the way, transporting a spoon full of

Chapter 3 My nighttime shelters

soup to my mouth was often unsuccessful. My hands were defying my control. It felt like everyone was watching me. I was hungry, so I had to eat the soup. Instead, I looked on my soup standing in front of me only to finally leave the table without eating, as hungry as before, feeling embarrassed and helpless.

Time passed slowly and I was still struggling with a lack of a warm, dry and safe place to stay. I was still looking. I looked into basements, sneaked into construction sites, checked various nooks and crannies. Even if I found something, it was all temporary and often dangerous. Public toilets, without service but usually heated, sometimes offered some comfort. Unfortunately, I could only stand there during the day and warm up a little. It was impossible to sleep there. They were closed at night, there was very little space inside and they were terribly uncomfortable. Sometimes, though, I managed to lock myself in a cubicle, lay on the floor curled up around the toilet, and take a nap. The toilets had another advantage – they had a washing basin. Although the water was cold, I could wash and even shave. I would wash my hair in cold water and go out into the freezing cold. After a while my hair would freeze and I had a cap of ice on my head. To this day I wonder how I survived it all? I had ice either on my head or on my feet.

Once, when looking for some accommodation, I spotted an old camping trailer parked in the same place perhaps for ages. I got the courage and grabbed the door handle. The door was open. I went inside. In the dark I was able to see a tattered table and a cupboard, but the best thing was the sofa, really nice and soft.

It was cold inside, but it was one of the better nights I've ever had when living on the street. I decided quickly. The next day, well before the *Herz As* soup kitchen opened, I was at the door. I wanted to be the first in the queue for the clothing delivery room. I knew that in *Herz As* you could get not only clean clothes, but also some household items. When I was inside, I asked if they had a sleeping bag. They didn't, but they offered me a quilt. I sat at the table until closing time. Sipping coffee, every now and then I looked at my treasure in a big bag. In my imagination, I saw myself in my trailer, on the soft sofa and under a warm duvet. I waited until the night came, walking up the nearby streets with the quilt in my hand and watching people and cars passing by. Finally I decided it was safe and jumped into the trailer. My first thought was to take off my shoes. Walking all day in the snow I got my shoes completely soaked. My feet were burning. It was unbearable. Even when I was drunk, my ever-wet feet hurt and itched terribly all the time. I wanted to get rid of those shoes, but I didn't have any to change, and in such weather I had to wear something. For many days and nights I couldn't take them off my feet.

Now I was in my trailer. I dropped the hated wet shoes and hid under the covers. It was warm and blissful, my legs were resting. But only until dawn.

I decided that I would only come here at night and sneak out of the trailer at dawn when nobody was around. I didn't want to lose the trailer, so I couldn't allow anyone to see me coming in or out of it. Should that happen, my appearance would alert the people and they would surely drive me away.

When I scrambled out from under the warm and comfortable covers the following morning, I was greeted by bitter frost inside the trailer. I reached for my shoes but they were like two blocks of ice. 'What to do? I have to get away.' I had no choice. I put my aching feet in the frozen shoes and left the trailer. After some time, the ice melted. Although the shoes were getting softer every minute, they were getting wetter, too. This situation happened again and again over the next days. I decided not to take my shoes off at night. I thought, 'Better if they dry up on my legs when I sleep.'

The other day I was walking around near the stadium where I used to sleep. In fact it wasn't far from my trailer. It was raining. I took shelter under the canopy of the closed stadium ticket offices. It was a good day – I had a 2-liter bottle of wine with me. I sat down under the roof, leaning my back against the door of an office, and occasionally took a pull from the bottle. Suddenly the door behind me gave way under the push of my back and ... I fell inside. The ticket office was empty. There was only a table, a chair, and an electric heater under the table. I thought, 'If this office is always open, I can stay here too.' I still had my trailer, but I decided that one day I would definitely 'check in' the empty office. I could treat it as my emergency place of accommodation. Provided it will stay open – the end of winter was close and another football season was about to begin. I was afraid that after the first match of the season someone could lock the door of my ticket office.

The trailer helped me to survive the most severe frosts during the winter. However, the evening came when I saw the empty space where it had been parked. I don't know when the trailer had been taken away, but it was gone with all my belongings, which I had collected and stored inside. My precious quilt, some old clothes pulled out of donation containers, shaving razors obtained in charities, pieces of soap and some other things. Everything was lost.

When my trailer disappeared and I was wondering where I would sleep, I remembered the ticket office near the *FC St Pauli* stadium. May it be open. As it turned out later, I found another warm haven there.

Is there any hope yet?

> *Your life will hang in suspense and you will stand in dread both day and night, never sure of your life. In the morning you will say, "Would that it were evening!" and in the evening you will say, "Would that it were morning!" because of the dread that your heart must feel and the sight that your eyes must see.*

Deuteronomy 28:66–67

I have not been idle during my winter rambles. I was looking for shelters all the time. I checked everything: the ruins of old buildings, trash cans, basements, various dark corners, bridges, and even thickets, or abandoned cars. I once found a truck with soft sofas in which I spent many nights over a couple of months.

In the spring I already had several places in various neighborhoods of Hamburg that were suitable for sleeping. I didn't use them before because it was too cold. It was getting warmer now so I could spread my wings.

In spring everything came back to life. The most important for me was a return to nightlife in *St. Pauli*. Warm nights, more people having fun, and what came with it – richer loot.

On the one hand, I was already well acquainted with the street living. I was able to find something to eat and drink, find a place to get some sleep or a facility where I could wash. On the other hand, however, I lived in increasing fear. Whom and what was I afraid of? I do not know. I was definitely scared of people. The way I looked often provoked aggression. I was severely beaten several times just because I was a homeless drunkard. What is more, I was afraid that someone would catch me sleeping in some illegal place. My

Chapter 3 My nighttime shelters

sleep was always a nap, during which I reacted to any noise nearby. Who will count how many hours I napped in such a way under bridges, particularly dangerous places?

Although I became aggressive if confronted, I was very afraid of the police. During the day I was afraid of assault. At night that someone will discover my hideout. In the morning, when I sobered up a bit, I was afraid to cross a street because I thought that a car would hit me. Anxiety, constant trembling all over my body and, alternately, sweating hot and freezing cold. Dirty clothes, insects and stench, 'Will I go on like that any longer?'

And this terrifying loneliness! How badly I needed someone who would understand me. My attempts to get closer to people made me aware of my situation. Everyone seemed to be running away. When I got on the subway train, there was a lot of empty space around me. Everyone backed away. Nobody needed me. From the faces of people passing by I could read, 'What is he still alive for?' Was there anyone in the world who didn't loathe me? Would anyone dare to touch me without disgust?

Months had passed since my last physical contact with people. These were doctors and nurses in a hospital. Namely, the other day I felt very, very bad. Something wrong was going on with me. Since the very morning I had problems with breathing. I slid down to the basement, where my den was at the time, to rest a bit. It was so bad that I just lay there and waited to either get better or die. I really wanted to fall asleep and never wake up again. Pain in the chest was growing and every breath I took ached worse and worse. I was short of air. I didn't want die in such pain. I crawled outside and almost on all fours reached the first bar asking for rescue. Then I passed out.

Henryk Krzosek GOD FOUND ME ON THE STREET

When I came round, I was inside an ambulance. I realized I had an oxygen mask on the face. Some people were leaning over me. I saw everything blurred. Some movements, some voices. Then the ceilings of the long corridors along which I was transported... and that was it. To this day I don't know how long I was unconscious. An hour? A day? Or maybe longer? When I woke up I discovered I was in a hospital bed. There was an IV connected to my arm. Something heavy rested on my feet. I was coming back to myself. Still every breath made me ache. I wanted to sleep, but I couldn't. Every now and then, a nurse would come in with a new ice pack to put on my legs. A change of IV. And there was only one heard repeatedly, *Fieber. Fieber. Fieber.* Night came. My constant struggle for every breath and the repeated actions of the nurses. On the third day, I received an injection. I felt so good after it! The pain subsided. I could breathe again. It felt blissful and so good.

Suddenly full awareness of what was happening to me returned. I looked around the room. On a chair by my bed lay my clothes. What a shame! All these dirty rugs! What was even worse, the nurses were wrapping my dirty legs with ice. They were taking off my filthy clothes, stinking socks. I wanted to run away, but I was still pinned to the IV. When the door opened, I pretended to be asleep. I survived like that until the next day while plotting an escape plan. Embarrassment and thirst, which came of the blue, strongly motivated me to take a desperate step. When the neighbor from the bed next to me came out of the ward, I pulled the needle out of my forearm, threw off my hospital shirt, dressed in my dirty clothes and went out on to the terrace. The room in which I was placed was on the ground floor. I walked from the terrace over the railing, into the park surrounding the hospital and from there into the street. I

Chapter 3 My nighttime shelters

was free! I left the shame behind. Now all I needed was a drink!

It wasn't long before I found out that I was not so repulsive to everyone. One hot day I was sitting on a bench in a park. As I watched people walking by and children playing on the grass, my thoughts returned to my family and children. 'Do they know what has become out of me? What I am going through?' I wondered what their reaction would be if they saw me like that? Is there anything else I can do for them and for myself? Various thoughts began to run through my mind. The strongest was that of suicide. 'Why do I live? There is no one in the world for whom I would matter.' No one would even notice if I disappeared from this world at that point. And just when I was thinking about my existence, a man sat down on next to me. On the same bench.

Why did he sit down on that bench? Didn't he see who I was? After all, my appearance said it all. Other benches nearby were empty. After a while the man took out a packet of cigarettes and offered me one. He didn't seem to feel disgusted! This was more I could take. I yearned so much for the presence of another normal person. Now an apparently well-to-do gentleman was sitting next to me, offering me a cigarette. He did not detest me. To avoid crying out loud, I picked myself up and walked away as quickly as I could. Only years later did I realize that in critical situations God always sent some angel to me. Meeting this man gave me hope. Unfortunately, it was only for a moment.

Chapter 4

God steps in

For the Son of Man has come to seek and to save what was lost.

Luke 19:10

TWO YEARS of rambling behind me. Two cold winters that I must have survived by some kind of miracle. Constant escapes, fear, hunger, drunkenness, vermin. I had had enough!

I went to a store with sailing supplies. I wanted to know the price of a thin but strong rope. I needed one that would not let me down. In the past, I wanted to hang myself on some string which unfortunately didn't hold up and broke at the most important moment.

This time it was supposed to be different. In the shop it turned out though that I could not afford the line. Selling empty bottles I was able to get some petty cash, but the price I saw was kind of astronomical. You know – a branded product. At that time in *Baumwall* (a harbor area of Hamburg) there were many stores with nautical equipment and accessories. I checked in which of them I could steal the rope I needed. In one of the stores I found a basket standing between racks and display cases, with all kinds of tourist souvenirs and ropes of different thickness. It was something for me. The problem was that very few customers would come to this store. If I just walked in, just like that, I would immediately draw attention.

Baumwall is a popular tourist destination in Hamburg. Everything there was cheap, except for the stuff from the stores offering professional equipment, which was exactly what my target was. On Saturdays and Sundays *Baumwall* was full with tourists. A multitude of people wandered from store to store. This was an opportunity for me. To mingle with a group of visitors and steal a piece of rope unnoticed. However, I had to improve my appearance. So I went to the soup kitchen. I stood in line for clean clothes, then I took a shower and shaved and I was ready for action. With some group of tourists I entered the nautical store I had selected before. From the basket I took the desired line. For a moment I looked as if I was going towards the checkout, but I just moved between the racks, the rope landed under my shirt and after a while I was back on the street.

My end was coming. Now I just had to find the right time. There was not much of a problem with the venue, because the basement, where I had lived for a long time, was perfect for that. There were sewage pipes under the ceiling, which begged for a rope to be hanged on them. A bucket of garbage could serve as a stand.

The bigger problem was with finding the right moment. It so happened that at that time I could easily find a way to get drunk. If not friends from the street, then some earned cash. I was drunk all the time. In such circumstances, I put off my suicide plans every day until the next day. I had the rope hidden behind the waistband and I was still waiting for the longed-for day. When the morning of 'tomorrow' came, I would wake up with a massive hangover. If I didn't have any

Chapter 4 God steps in

alcohol at hand, my thoughts went in one direction, 'Where to get a quick drink to start functioning?'

Days and weeks passed, and with a rope under my belt, I was still in the same place. Until finally, the day came. I couldn't find any alcohol. I quickly decided. Today was the end of me! With that mindset, I went to the kitchen one more time. One last meal. With it I will gain some strength and say goodbye to the world.

This particular soup kitchen where I dropped in before death differed from other facilities of this kind. All the workers were dressed in uniforms, and while we were eating, someone from the staff was all the time talking to us about God. To start the meal, someone was praying. Someone was reading something. In my condition, I didn't really understand what it was all about. Although there was a big sign hanging in front of the entrance to the cafeteria: *Die Heilsarmee*, which, as I later learned, means The Salvation Army. We, the homeless of Polish descent, called the soup kitchen simply 'Jesus'. We would say, 'Let's eat something at Jesus'.'

Die Heilsarmee – The Salvation Army. Who planned it so that an oasis of salvation could be found in the city of debauchery – as *St. Pauli* is called – among porn cinemas, erotic-entertainment establishments, in the neighborhood of prostitution, drugs, alcoholism and crime? Do slogans like *'JESUS LEBT!'* – 'Jesus lives!' or *'JESUS IN ST. PAULI'* in a place like that have any meaning? For over twenty years I have known that they do, because it is in this place that I have received new life.

But let's come back to my plans. It is June 1989. I am sitting hunched over at the table in the soup kitchen. The tightness of the rope around my waist reminds me of what I have planned to do. In truth, I didn't want to die at all... but I didn't know how to live either. At some point I looked at the wall in front of me. There was and a poster hanging there with a sentence in Polish, saying:

> *For God so loved the world that he gave his only Son, so that everyone who believes in him might not perish but might have eternal life.* (John 3:16)

Whenever I went there, I would read this short passage. I don't even know when I learned the text by heart. I never thought about its meaning. I just read it because it was in my language. But now the words on the poster began to speak to me in some strange way. Does what is on the poster have any meaning for me? 'God loved the world.' I am still in the world. Does this mean that God loves me too? 'That whoever believes in Him should not perish but have life.' Does God at all exist? As a child I went to church, to religion classes. And what did that get me? Nothing! I must die! If He exists, does He want me to live? Above the entrance to the soup kitchen was a sign, *JESUS LEBT*. Is Jesus really alive?

Still preoccupied with my thoughts, I asked the staff lady to bring me a plate of soup. In doing so, I broke the rules of the kitchen, because here everyone was supposed to walk up to the table where the soup pots stood to get their meal. I knew, however, that in my condition I was unable to carry the soup myself. The woman easily agreed to help me. After a while she came to the table with the soup for me, and something else. Next to the plate she put a booklet in Polish entitled *Alcohol and family*. She asked me to read it and added,

'Henryk, only God can help you!'

How did she know that right at that moment I was thinking about my problems and... about God?

Chapter 4 God steps in

I didn't want to read it at first. I could already tell by the title what was inside. Me, an alcoholic who had wrecked his family. I knew that was the case. Why else would I read about it? On the other hand, I thought, here comes an opportunity for me to finally read something in Polish. I ate my soup. I took the booklet and went to a nearby park. I sat on a bench and read.

A moment later I was crying like a sore thumb. The booklet contained testimonies of alcoholics who had found freedom through prayer and God's intervention. I read it in its entirety. Could I also benefit from it? I didn't yet know if what I read was true. Does God exist? I won't know unless I try. I need to pray. But how does one do that?

I couldn't remember any prayers from the past. I didn't have any prayer book. The rope behind my belt kept pressing. 'God! If you exist, I don't want to die! If it is true what I've just read, give me freedom from alcohol, just like you did to these people.' That was my first prayer.

What happened next? I managed five days *without* alcohol. God began a process of transformation in me.

It may seem to someone that five days without drinking is nothing special. For me, who for two years was thinking every day only about one thing, how to get drunk, it was something incredible. Somewhere inside me I felt that God was somehow answering my prayer. Something new began to happen in me. I began to fight. I moved out of *St. Pauli*. I stopped visiting those places where I could drink. I stopped visiting soup kitchens too.

I was devastated by a terrible hangover, but I tried with all my might to fight back. One day. Two days. Instead of getting better – it was getting worse. On the third day, the horrible mood was joined by ravenous hunger. When I was drinking I could even not eat anything and I was fine. Now, when I gave up alcohol, my stomach demanded more and more food. One more day. Somehow I was able to stand, but I felt it was beyond my strength.

On the fifth day, all my motivation to fight melted away. I gave up. I came back to *St. Pauli*, to my friends from the street. To my previous state. To the rope that I still carried around my waist. In my heart I said to myself, 'There is no God.'

After a few days I was again sitting at a table of the kitchen 'At Jesus'.' There was that woman again. She asked me if I had read the booklet. I told her about my five-day unsuccessful struggle. Although I had already given up the fight and my attempts to believe in God, I asked her if there wasn't something more about faith in Polish? She said she would look for it. After a while she came back and handed me some materials with information about God and different churches. Among them was one tiny booklet entitled 'Have You Heard of the Four Laws of Spiritual Life?' This booklet was the smallest and the thinnest. The largest, or rather the thickest book she brought me too was 'The New Testament.' As it turned out later, these two books – the thinnest and the thickest – had a tremendous impact on my subsequent life. I will start with the smallest.

Already on the first page I learned the first truth: God loves me! There I found the text from the poster, which I already knew by heart, *'For God so loved the world that he gave his only Son, so that everyone who believes in Him should not perish but have eternal life.'*[1] Even though I could be denying this considering all my experiences, I had to fully agree with another truth I learned from this booklet: I was a sinner! I was beginning to understand something. I, a sinner,

---

[1] John 3:16

Chapter 4 God steps in

cannot unite with the Holy God. That was probably why I didn't feel Him care. I have to do something about it. But what? For five days I wanted to do something real, I fought to become a better person... and nothing came out of it. The explanation of this failure came with the third truth from the booklet: by my own powers I can never make it, I can never come closer to God. That is why He sent His Son Jesus to me. For my sins I should die, and that is what I was aiming for. Meanwhile, God sent Jesus so that He would die for me and I would live. I felt I was beginning to understand, but then I still didn't know what. The fourth truth spoke of the need to accept Jesus Christ into your life – through prayer. And an example of prayer was given. I finally knew how to pray! 'This will be my prayer!' – I decided.

> **Lord Jesus. I need You. I acknowledge my sinfulness. I open the door of my life to You and accept You as my Savior and Lord. I thank You that You forgave my sins by dying on the cross for me. I ask for Your guidance in my life. Make me the kind of person You want me to be.**

Did anything change in my life after that prayer? At first I thought nothing had changed. I continued to steal and drink. But I found myself thinking about God more and more often. At such moments I would sit down on a bench and take out of my pocket the thickest book I got at the soup kitchen – the New Testament. I read about Jesus. I didn't understand everything, but I kept on reading. The story of Jesus began to fascinate me more and more. The stories with the lepers, with the woman caught on adultery, with the hungry, with the sick. He was helping everyone! Something was happening in me. Some kind of hope was being born. 'Maybe all is not yet lost,' I thought. Then I would take out my second book and read my prayer.

When I got to the tenth chapter of John's Gospel in the New Testament, to the end of the tenth verse, and when I read that Jesus came that the sheep *'might have life and have it more abundantly'*,[2] the thought of throwing away the rope came into my head. 'Wait, wait, Henryk! Nothing has changed after all. Don't throw away what you've struggled to gain', something inside me resisted strongly.

Still with the rope by my belt, still drunk, I read my New Testament. Jesus came into the world to die for me? I couldn't understand it. How could Jesus die for *me*? After all, I was born two thousand years after His death? Something didn't add up. I left that question for later. Something else caught my attention: I read that Jesus' body was not found in the tomb – He had risen from the dead. Then he began to appear in various places. Could this be true? Is Jesus really alive? Let's assume that yes – Jesus is alive. Then where can we meet him? If He is alive, is He the same as the Gospels describe Him? If He is alive and the same, can He help me? These and other thoughts troubled me constantly. Hungover or drunk, I was thinking about Jesus. I wanted to meet Him.

It had been a few weeks since I had started reading the New Testament and asking myself questions about Jesus when suddenly on the street someone stuck a flyer in my hand. As far as I could tell, an evangelistic event was to take place on the square where my trailer used to stand, next to the *St. Pauli* stadium, in my area, and it was to start on the 6th of July and last for the next four days. I didn't really understand the word 'evangelistic' at the time, but further down in the flyer I read that it was to be 'an encounter with

---
[2] John 10:10

Chapter 4 God steps in

the living Jesus who frees, heals and transforms people's lives.' The invitation was directed to everyone, but especially to 'those who have problems with addictions, illnesses or other life problems.' I thought I had to be there. There were only a few days left until July 6. I mobilized myself a lot, I even limited my drinking for fear that I might miss the meeting. Finally the long awaited day came. I was already excited from the very morning. I didn't even drink much, although I had the opportunity, because as it turned out later, my other friends from the street had also drawn to the evangelism. Some of them were well supplied. Circling around the square I kept running into buddies well equipped with bottled beverages.

Somewhere under my skin I felt that on that day I must somehow refrain from drinking. The evangelization was supposed to start at 4 p.m. and I had been walking around the square since morning. I watched as benches were being set up, a stage was being built, tents were being raised and loudspeakers were being placed around. A band was rehearsing on the stage. This filled me with a kind of hope. I didn't know why, but I had a feeling that this was the right place for me, and that something would happen today.

As the time passed, there was more and more people in the square. I watched everything from a safe distance. More and more people were filling the seats around the stage. They were coming from all directions. The musicians finally installed themselves on the stage and a concert started. The music was different from anything I had ever heard before. It didn't fit in with my favorite rock genre – although there were guitars and drums. It also didn't match the music I had heard in church on other occasions. And this was a religious event, after all. 'What is the point of all this? Why does this music almost send shivers through my body?'

Henryk Krzosek ❧ GOD FOUND ME ON THE STREET

A month earlier I had attended another event. One of the greatest rock bands in the world, *Pink Floyd*, were on tour in Hamburg. As a young man I was their great fan. In my previous life, while back in Poland, I possessed all their records, for which I had spent a fortune. To see them live in concert I would have paid even more. Now it was close to come true. The concert was to take place in *Stadtpark*. 'But how to get there?' I couldn't afford a ticket. 'I'm sure I will work something out' – I thought. I got to the venue a long time before it began. I wanted to check out all the opportunities to sneak into the audience without a ticket.

At first glance, I had little chance. Everything was separated by a high metal fence. Behind the fence, every few meters stood a menacing-looking guard. Police everywhere. I comforted myself with the fact that even if I had no chance to see anything, at least I could listen to the concert from behind the fence. I went to the nearest store and – to console myself – stole a bottle of wine. While I was waiting for things to start, some punk gave me a treat of a joint. I'd never smoked weed before, but this random guy convinced me it was better than my wine.

I drank some wine, smoked some weed. In order to hear everything clearly I got to the very fence. On the other side of the fence, which was inaccessible to me, were thousands of people. But thousands were also on my side. When the music came from the stage, something unbelievable happened: the crowd pushed against the fence, which immediately collapsed. I also happened to be in this crowd. The interventions of security guards and stewards were futile. As I later read in a newspaper, about three thousand people forced their way through the fence to the concert as 'stowaways.' In this way my old dream came true. I was there, at a concert of my favorite band, right in front of the stage. Although I

Chapter 4 God steps in

was drunk and high, my experience was unforgettable, so much so that the next day after the concert I stole a cassette of the band's live recording from a music store. I have no idea why I did it, because I didn't have any device to play it on. But I carried it with me for a very long time.

An evangelistic concert vs. a *Pink Floyd* concert. And the abyss between them. But the music I was hearing now in the square sounded much better to me. It brought some warmth to my inner self and even more hope that something would happen today.

The prayer

The main part of the program started. In order not to draw attention with my appearance, I sat in the last row on a bench under a tree. Music was flowing from the stage and – I don't know why – I was crying. A very famous Protestant preacher, Reinhard Bonke, appeared on the stage. He spoke about the love of God. About the fact that Jesus is in this place and will heal. This was all new to me. I didn't know what I was taking part in. I didn't understand German very well, but I felt what was being said. I wanted someone to explain it all to me. I didn't want to miss a word. I was convinced that this was my chance. I tried to pray. I wanted to say the 'Our Father,' but I couldn't remember the words. I fell apart completely. I cried and cried. The rope around my waist was pressing more and more, and I kept begging Jesus to do something with me.

At one point, someone came up to me and asked what was wrong with me? What was I supposed to answer? I threw out my answer as best I could, in German, 'I am a homeless alcoholic. I am hungry. I sleep in a dumpster. I came here to pray that Jesus would change my life.' Suddenly other people appeared around me. They were all interested in me as if I was of great value. They suggested that I come with them closer to the stage from which this famous preacher was speaking. I did. I saw also other people getting up from their seats and walking in the same direction. I realized that the prayer had begun. The people who had brought me to the front put their hands on me and began to pray. I prayed with them. Best I could.

I remember my prayer. It was very short: 'Lord Jesus. If you are here, change my life. I never want to drink again. If You are not there, I will hang myself.' Nothing more. While others were still praying over me, a feeling like fire went through my body. I seemed to be burning. Sweat began to pour down on me. It flooded my eyes. 'What are they doing to me? I'm about to fall!' Fortunately, they finished the prayer. I felt very tired. I said I had to go now. I was suggested to come again tomorrow. They would be waiting for me.

Exhausted, I hid in my dumpster in the basement. I fell fast asleep. When I woke up in the morning and came out of the dungeon into the daylight, I found out that I felt somewhat strange, somehow different. The fear, which had been my companion for a long time, seemed to have vanished. I was no longer afraid to cross the street. Then I saw a group of my buddies standing outside a 24/7 convenience store. They were perching on the stairs and one of them was opening a two-liter bottle of the cheapest wine.

We, the homeless, had our own meeting venues. We always met in different places, without any prior arrangement. We helped each other. Today I have some booze to share, tomorrow someone else will have. This way we would get at least a sip of beer to start the day somehow. One of such

Chapter 4 God steps in

places was near this store. Seeing me walk by, they began calling me to join them. But I did not feel *any* need to drink. Whatsoever! 'What is going on?' I would have never before turned down such an opportunity. And suddenly I discovered that I didn't want to drink at all! I passed the companions and went away, heading to the park.

I sat down on a bench, took some tobacco from my pocket and started to roll a cigarette. And there was a new discovery. While rolling, my hands were not shaking. I began to analyze everything. 'Yesterday I was prayed for. I also prayed that Jesus would change my life. Today no hangover. I refused to drink. And now I've rolled perhaps the most beautiful cigarette of my life, with steady hands. What's all this? Did God hear yesterday's prayer? If so, then, 'Lord God. Make me not smoke too.' The cigarette I smoked then turned out to be my last one.

I paced the streets for hours and wondered about what was happening to me. I couldn't find an explanation. But I trusted that the people who had prayed for me yesterday would also be able to explain. 'But would I meet them today?' The flyer said that this evangelization would continue for three more days. On that day it was also to begin at 4 p.m. How time flew by slowly. I couldn't wait to meet the people I met the day before.

It started to rain. Such weather made my situation complicated. 'Even if I can now hide from the rain somewhere under a roof, what will I do at an open-air event? I don't have any clothes to change. Have to choose: either I cancel the meeting and wait out the rain somewhere hidden, or I go to the meeting and get soaked.' I chose the latter. Even if I get soaked, I will walk around all night to let my clothes dry on me.

Henryk Krzosek ❧ GOD FOUND ME ON THE STREET

When the long-awaited hour was approaching, slowly, hiding under any roof I could, I was striving to get to the square. On the way, I heard music in a distance, which attracted me. And I walked closer. I still liked listening to music, although lately I didn't have such an opportunity very often. I wondered where the music came from. It turned out that on *Spielbudenplatz* (as the German name suggests – a place where gaming pavilions were located) a new pavilion was being opened – *'Spielothek'*. For this reason, a promoting feast was being celebrated in front of the facility. In front of the pavilion there was a canopy and set up tables. You could get a free sausage, some cake and a coffee, and the whole event was accompanied by a music band. I took advantage of this opportunity in two ways: I could take shelter from the rain and eat something. Then a woman came out of the pavilion carrying a bunch of umbrellas and started handing them out to everyone around. In this way I obtained a big white umbrella. The rain was no longer a threat to me. At the evangelistic event, where I was heading, I could protected from the rain not only myself but also the interpreter, who had been invited for me by the people I had met the previous day.

When I told the interpreter (I was very happy to have him by my side) how I got the umbrella, he declared that it was God who took care of me that I would not have to walk around in wet clothes. Until then I had never heard of God taking care of an umbrella for some homeless person in the rain.

On that day, the first day of my not drinking, I began to believe that God was real. He was hearing my prayer: I didn't drink, I didn't smoke, and I had somebody to translate for me only. I was getting anything what I asked for. And

Chapter 4 God steps in

on top of that, He added an umbrella. That was how the second day of my meeting with God went by.

The third day was sunny. My interpreter gave me a Bible with his dedication. He also said that it was very important for me to join a church. He was the pastor of Ahrensburg Baptist Church and invited me to join. I thought this was a little strange because these other people I had just met said exactly the same thing. It was as if they were colluding. Everyone was offering me some kind of church. I already carried several flyers in my pockets inviting me to visit one church or another. I didn't understand why there were so many churches. I thought there was only one Catholic Church. I had heard something about Protestants, but I didn't know who they were or where they came from. When I was proposed to join some church, I kept saying, 'I am a Catholic.' The people were helpless. My problem was that this great evangelistic event had been organized and carried out by various non-Catholic denominations. Baptists, Methodists, Pentecostals, Evangelicals, Free Churches – and among them me, a Catholic in need.

At the end of that third day, one of the guys who had somehow taken care of me from the beginning brought me a flyer with a hand-written name on it: *Iwona Madziar*. He informed me that the girl was taking part in that event, that she was Polish, and that she belonged to the Catholic Church. That day's meeting was already coming to an end, so he suggested that I would find her somewhere there the following day. Maybe she would be able to give me some further help.

The next day I began my search. First of all, I was looking for the boy who had told me about Iwona. I thought he would help me find the Catholic girl. Apparently, my mentor did not attend the event on that day and my search was unsuccessful. Being on my own, I was losing hope as time went by. I thought, 'How can I find her among these crowds? I have no chance.'

The evangelization event was officially over. The crowd started to disperse. Only the cleaning crews remained on the venue. The benches were being taken. The stage and tents surrounding the whole square were being dismantled. The event in which I had actively participated for four days finally came to an end. 'What will happen to me now? Should I return to my previous life?' Full of disappointment and doubts I entered the one still standing big tent. There were some people inside. They were packing books into cardboard boxes. I saw a young girl with a badge on her blouse. I timidly came closer. On the badge I read: *Iwona Madziar*.

My heart jumped. It was her! It was her I was looking for. 'But how to begin? How to talk to her?' I took the flyer with her name out of my pocket and walked over to her. I said fearfully that I had received the leaflet from somebody and that the guy said that if I found a person with that name she would help me. Iwona asked me what kind of help I needed. I said that I was a homeless alcoholic and that I was sleeping in a dumpster. 'I haven't had a drink for three days now. I have nothing and nobody to help me. I don't know what to do with myself anymore.' She was probably surprised by what I told her. She went away to talk to a group of people. I think they had some sort of consultation. When she returned, she offered to pray. I was seated on a bench and surrounded by a circle of people. They stretched their hands over me and prayed. I didn't understand what it was all about, but I blubbered again like a baby. After the prayer, Iwona proposed a meeting, 'Tomorrow at *Hauptbahnhof*'.

Chapter 5
A new beginning

So whoever is in Christ is a new creation: the old things have passed away; behold, new things have come.

2 Corinthians 5:17

I DIDN'T think that Iwona would come. I might have assumed that she made an appointment with me, just to get rid of me. I waited for her at the appointed time. To my great surprise she came. She bought me something to eat and started inquiring about my situation. After quickly figuring out my entire life situation, she said that I was definitely eligible for some sort of social security benefit. When I told her that I didn't have any documents to get anything from the authorities, she decided that we had to try anyway. We started at the identification office, which was right next to the station. Iwona helped me a lot, also financially, so I was able to get have the photo done quickly. I filled in the appropriate form and was supposed to report again at the appointed time. One thing was settled. But what next? Iwona decided that we would go to *Arbeitsamt*, the labor office. She didn't care about my grumbling that it was not worth trying without an ID, that there was no chance for anything and so on. To tell the truth, back then, this young student was someone who decided about my fate. I was very surprised that I had given her such power over me, but under my skin I felt that this was the way it should be. The future will prove that I was right.

The next morning I waited for Iwona outside the office and she did not show up. I thought it was even better, because we wouldn't get anything done anyway. I was about to leave when Iwona appeared from around the corner. She excused her being late and started to act right away. She quickly found the right floor and the right room. I don't know with what attitude Iwona entered the office, but mine was totally negative. No hope. After all, it was about money and I had no documents.

Iwona started a conversation with a clerk and at the very beginning she told her that I did not have any document. Eventually, Iwona became our interpreter. The clerk asked me about various details. When I came to Germany, when I was registered for the first time at the labor office, whether I had received unemployment benefits before, how long I had been without any benefits. Finally, she asked if I really didn't have any document with my name on it? I remembered that I did have something with my name on it. It was a certificate from prison stating that I had been employed there while serving my sentence. Ashamed, I took out the crumpled and dirty paper and handed it to Iwona, and Iwona passed it to the clerk who handled our case. The woman called the prison and after a short conversation decided to issue me with a certificate of one-time social assistance, assuring me that once the office had issued me with an identity document, I would be entitled to a permanent social benefit.

Later that day we went to the social security office to pick up the money for me. I did not understand what had

Chapter 5 A new beginning

happened. No documents. No address. No language skills. In a scrupulous – when it comes to regulations – German office I got the money. To put it briefly, God must have had his fingers in it.

Although I already had some money, I still spent the night in a dumpster. I was stunned. I had a lot of money – the whole amount of 360 marks! I was afraid of them! What would happen to me if I couldn't count on Iwona's help? With so much money on me, I could easily give in to temptation and go into a liquor store. I decided that I would leave myself a few pennies and I would deposit most of the money with Iwona. I asked her to help me manage my resources. Iwona left me her phone number and we parted. A few days later I had a document confirming my identity and on its basis I applied for an ID. Everything worked fine.

Then Iwona said that she was taking me to a meeting of her community, whom I had already met partially during the evangelization concert. The meeting was also to be attended by the pastor of the parish to which the community belonged. This priest had already declared that he would offer me some help. Before the meeting I asked Iwona if I could buy myself some cheap shoes. The ones I had on my feet were in a terrible condition. Iwona agreed and gave me the amount I needed.

I still didn't understand anything of this! Until now nobody had decided about my expenses. I hadn't even given my wife that right. I was always able to hide something for myself. It was completely different with Iwona. Why did this young student girl, whom I had just met, gain my trust? I constantly felt that I had to listen to her and submit to her decisions. Maybe it's strange, but with Iwona I felt like a child, and I saw in her – although much younger than me – something like a mother.

We were going to my first prayer meeting. On the way there, Iwona was explaining to me what such a meeting is about, who comes and where it takes place. Once we were at the meeting, someone asked me to talk about what was happening to me. For a long while I spoke and Iwona translated it into German. When I finished my story, the pastor offered to pray for me. Just like under a tent, they sat me down in the middle, the pastor and someone else put their hands on me and prayed. And I... cried again. After the prayer, a conversation started about how to help me.

The pastor of the Catholic Parish of St. Wilhelm, Father Joachim von Stockhausen, decided that I no longer return to the dumpster at *St. Pauli*, but that I live with him in the parish house. He said he had a room in the basement where I could arrange a tiny apartment for myself. Then Dorota, whom I had met with her husband Peter in the tent, said that she would take care of the bedding for me. Another woman said that if I stayed there she would bring me some clothes the following day. After a while the conversation turned to the topic of a job. I was to receive my identity card in a few days. Now I had only a certificate that I was waiting for the ID. Unfortunately, there was no place of residence on that certificate or on the ID I was soon to receive. I was still a homeless person, and this complicated the possibility of finding a job quickly. The leaders of the community, Dr. Norbert Friedrich and his wife, Ilze, offered to register me at their address. Things were starting to look up.

When I received my ID, there was already a correction on it: instead of *Ohne festen Wohnsitz*, which translates to 'Without permanent residence,' there was my first registered German address of residence. 'Oh, God! Am I dreaming? In just a few days, such great changes in my life. God! You listen to all my requests. I think I feel that You love me!'

Chapter 5 A new beginning

With such a prayer, for the first time in two years, I lay down in bed with white, clean sheets. I couldn't sleep. All the past was coming back to my mind: what I had been, what I had been doing, where I had been, what I had felt. 'Yesterday I was lying on a pile of wet cardboard. And today...'

There was a cross hanging on the wall opposite the bed. I got up, took it off the wall and, hugging it to myself, lay down again. 'Jesus! You died for me. I want to be with You always, forever.' At the age of thirty-eight, pressing the cross tighter and tighter to my chest, I felt truly loved for the first time in my life! I'm not even trying to describe it, because God's love goes beyond any description. I just felt love! Over the following days, when I was closing my eyes, I felt the presence of Jesus. There were times when I would wake up in the middle of the night. I did not open my eyes. I was afraid. 'What will happen if I open my eyes and see Jesus?'

Then we started a job hunt for me. Iwona, Ilse, Norbert and the others searched through job listings in newspapers. In one of them we found something: 'Cleaning, two hours a day, a grocery store'. Why not? Good to start with. I went to the store immediately and the following day I could start work. I agreed with the manager that I would come two hours before the opening or, if necessary, stay two hours after the closing of the store. A so-called 'basis job', for 420 marks a month.

I was happy to have the job, but it was kind of a joke. The shop that I was now working in was... a liquor store! Not so long before I would steal booze in shops like that. Now I was here alone. The manager was working somewhere in the back, and I was rearranging bottles while wiping dust. And believe me or not, it never crossed my mind to take a bottle from a shelf and open it.

Henryk Krzosek ◈ GOD FOUND ME ON THE STREET

While I was still looking for work, I was granted unemployment benefits. It all coincided with my first paycheck. Since I was earning my own money, I was no longer eligible for the welfare. But I did have the money. What is more, I needed it very much. But I decided to give it back. If I wanted to change, I had to change completely. I was more and more surprised by my own behavior. I didn't recognize myself. The values that had always been important to me were gone! And only a few weeks before, when I was homeless, I sometimes had some cash. When I had enough money for alcohol and some more, I would often go to a snack bar to order *Frikadellen*, kind of fried meatballs. One cost DM1.20. I liked them very much, but I never had enough money to eat to my heart's content.

When my first paycheck came I realized I had fair money in my pocket. Suddenly the thought came to me, 'Go to *St. Pauli* and eat as many meatballs as you wish, finally!' I got on the bus and got off near the snack bar. I decided to take only two meatballs to start with, so that I could later buy something else and eat to the full. When I was paying, I gave the server a note of twenty marks, and she gave me back change from fifty! 'Excuse me, ma'am. I gave you twenty marks only. You're giving me too much.' 'Oh, how kind of you!' she replied, 'How rare it is to meet such an honest man today.' I took the two *Frikadellen*, the right change, sat down at the table and began to wonder, 'Heniek[1], what has happened to you? It wasn't so long ago that you would have left those meatballs behind, and run away with that accidentally acquired money!'

---

[1] *Heniek* is a diminutive form of the first name *Henryk* (Eng. *Henry*), usually used among teen boys. Among adults, a colleague or friend would use this form to show closer relationship and lack of distance.

Chapter 5 A new beginning

I believe that then, when I was eating my meatballs, it was the first time God clearly spoke to me. 'You don't have to cheat anymore. I have changed your heart,' were exactly the words I heard somewhere inside of me. I was overwhelmed with joy, but I didn't know if it was because of the voice, or because of the good deed I had done to the woman. I just ate two meatballs and left.

The next morning I grabbed my Bible and opened it at random. I read a passage from the Book of Ezekiel, chapter thirty-six, verse twenty-six: '*I will give you a new heart, and a new spirit I will put within you. I will remove the heart of stone from your flesh and give you a heart of flesh.*' I thought, 'Does what I'm reading apply to me too? Does it have anything to do with my behavior yesterday at the snack bar and the voice I heard? Has God really given me a new heart? Do I no longer have to cheat, steal, and mess around?' It all fit together. I just needed some kind of confirmation that I was right. And a confirmation was soon to come.

After a month of my work in the grocery store, the manager gave me a more demanding task to do. I no longer wiped dust off the shelves, but was responsible for cleaning all the equipment in the food department. From that moment on, I worked only in the evenings, when the store was closed. It was not light work, but I was glad that the manager trusted me. My job now involved dismantling the machines for cleaning and reassembling them again.

My life was stable. I had a place to live. I went to work and earned my living. I attended meetings of the prayer community once a week. A very joyful existence. I still felt the strong presence of God, although He stopped working in a spectacular way. And I must admit that during that time I became accustomed to His work.

Henryk Krzosek ❧ GOD FOUND ME ON THE STREET

The other day at a prayer meeting the pastor came and gave me the address of a company and suggested that I look for a job as a welder there. The next day I went to the factory, with some anxiety in the heart. I entered the office and, in my poor German, I was trying to explain from whom I got the address and what I was looking for. The woman I spoke with called someone. After a short conversation, she showed me to another room on the first floor. The man who greeted me there asked in the beginning if I knew Fr. Joachim von Stockhausen. 'Of course I do, I'm staying in his house.' I think my answer settled the matter. The man I was talking to was the production manager. He asked about my education, whether I could weld and whether I had work clothes, because I could start work the same day. He said he would hire me for a trial period only, but if I did well, I would be employed on a permanent basis. We agreed that I would return the following day.

I went home and thought about how to handle all this. 'I already have one job, after all. And here comes another one, full-time and in my profession. What if I quit my job in the grocery, and then fail my trial period in the factory? What then?' Fortunately, I worked only in the evenings now, and in the new place I was supposed to work on the morning shift. I was able to manage. I started working in two jobs – one in the morning and the other in the evening.

After two weeks it became obvious to me that I had to quit the store. After talking to the manager, we agreed that I would work until the end of the month so that he could find someone to take my tasks.

When I came to the store for the last time, the women from the food department had prepared a gift for me, which was a real surprise – I was given a large bottle of expensive aftershave. One of the women said: 'Henryk, it's a shame

Chapter 5 A new beginning

you're leaving. We never had such a good employee.' Hearing this, I had exactly the same thoughts as previously in the snack bar. 'What happened? If only this woman knew about how I used to quit my jobs before, simply by abandoning a job or by being fired! God, is this your doing again? Did you actually give me a new heart?'

The first problems

> *Do not fear, for I have redeemed you;*
> *I have called you by name: you are mine.*
> *When you pass through waters, I will be with you;*
> *through rivers, you shall not be swept away.*
> *When you walk through fire, you shall not be burned,*
> *nor will flames consume you.*
>
> Isaiah 43:1b–2

When everything was meshing so beautifully and I felt God's presence at almost every turn, at some point a part of it ground to a halt. I had a secure job in my learned profession. I was meeting new believers in God who were giving me evidence of selfless friendship. I had everything I needed. Sweet life! And it was during that idyllic time that something in my new life began to creak. I had no idea that the time had come for me to confront my past. Although I had left my old life behind, I still had to face the consequences of my past actions. First, I had to take responsibility for all the thefts I had committed.

As a homeless person, I enjoyed a kind of 'privilege' of not having a criminal record. When I was caught stealing, I was released as soon as the police had written a report. My thefts were not so serious that I could be locked up right away. It was also impossible to sue me – I was not registered, so I could not be found and could not even be notified of the pending proceedings.

The situation changed radically when my address became officially known. The sender of the first letter that reached me at the address was the police. It was a subpoena. On a certain day, at a certain time, I was to appear at the police station for an interrogation. I was devastated. I had just started my probationary period at my new job, so I wanted to show my best side, and here this summons. 'What will my manager think of me when I tell him I have to go to the police instead of going to work? Will he still want an employee who has had a conflict with the law? I wanted to somehow hide my past from everyone, and there you go!

I called Iwona and asked her to call the police station on my behalf, where I was supposed to appear, and ask her to postpone the interview until the afternoon. Later Iwona told me that when the policeman she spoke to heard that I was asking to postpone the meeting because of work, he said that it was probably some kind of mistake. After all, the Henryk Krzosek whom he summoned would not able to do any work in his 'condition.' It was only after Iwona had explained everything that he agreed to postpone the interrogation.

I went to the police station with Iwona as my interpreter. So began the time of coming to terms with the past. The policeman was apparently surprised by my appearance, but he received us very politely. At the beginning he explained that he had been working on my case for a long time and all police information about me landed on his desk. By this time, he had accumulated thirteen theft charges that are

Chapter 5 A new beginning

subject to resolution by the court. He then informed me of each crime I was charged with and asked for an explanation.

I pleaded guilty to each crime charged. Because they were two types of theft – stealing alcohol and stealing food, my justification for committing these acts was very short and simple. I stole alcohol because I needed to drink, and food because I was hungry.

Iwona described the situation I was currently in. To confirm all this I showed the pay slip I had received. The policeman, who was more and more impressed by my change, promised that he would give a very positive opinion about my documents, but unfortunately, he had to send all the files to the court and the court would decide about my further fate. I had to wait for the message. Finally we shook hands. The policeman wished me good luck in my new life and said that we would meet again for sure, but he believed that it would be our last meeting in the roles of policeman and criminal.

After about two months another subpoena arrived. As before, I went the with Iwona. The policeman I knew explained only that due to the interest of the owners of the stores where I committed thefts, the court decided to sue me and he had to complete the files and give a final opinion about me. In doing so, he assured me that he would send the court a very good opinion about me. This was all he could do for me. For my part, I just have to wait for the summons.

And indeed the summons came shortly thereafter. The hearing was set for January 4, 1990. Exactly six months after my conversion. I wrestled with my thoughts about what would happen if the judge asked me whether I had committed any other thefts in addition to the charges listed in the indictment. If I denied, nothing would happen. The court had no evidence that I had done anything else. But then I would be lying, and after all, I made a decision not to lie anymore. However, if the court had had something else in the files, and I had told the truth and admitted it, then I would have gotten a bigger sentence. The internal struggle continued until the very last moment. Just before I entered the courtroom, I made a decision – I will not lie and I will confess to all the acts I have committed! 'Dear God, please help!'

I stood eye to eye with justice. The routine trial proceedings began. The indictment was read to me. And then came the first good news for me. The prosecutor had dropped thirteen theft charges, as was originally in the indictment I had received in the mail. He demanded that I be punished for four counts of theft – two cases of stealing alcohol and two cases of stealing meatballs.

The court accepted the request of the prosecutor. I was asked for some explanation as to why I had committed these acts. My explanation was again short, 'I stole alcohol because I was an alcoholic and without drinking I did not function, and I stole the meatballs because I was hungry.'

The judge then read the information collected about me, which stated that I was no longer homeless and had not been drinking for six months. That I was employed and my net monthly earnings were between 1700 and 1900 marks, that I was paying child support in the amount of 429 marks per month. All this had been documented in my files. The only thing missing was a the amount of rent. The judge wanted to supplement a document on this, so he asked me to provide the information. I explained that I was staying in the parish house and I didn't have to pay anything for accommodation. From what I heard next I could deduce that I was to face a fine, not imprisonment. 'The more expenses

Chapter 5 A new beginning

I have, the better for me,' – I thought. 'If I say I don't pay for the apartment, the fine might go up because I have more income, but then I'll lie. No, no, no! I won't be lying anymore!'

I told what my situation was. The judge described my truthful explanation in the minutes as follows: since I didn't pay anything for the apartment because I lived with a friend, the court would treat my situation as if I had been spending 300 marks a month for the apartment and would take this into account when imposing the sentence.

After some deliberation, the decision on the sentence was reached. I was found guilty of four thefts and sentenced to 90 days in prison with a fine of 30 marks per day, which amounted to 2700 marks, to be paid in monthly installments of 200 marks.

I was so happy when I left the court! It didn't matter that I had to pay two thousand seven hundred marks for two bottles of vodka and two packs of meatballs; the important thing was that I had put a piece of the past behind me. But the greatest joy of all was the certainty that during the trial, in addition to my public lawyer, the greatest defender of all was Jesus Christ standing by me. Though no one did see Him. No one heard His voice. He was with me just as He had promised:

> *When you pass through waters, I will be with you;*
> *through rivers, you shall not be swept away.*
> *When you walk through fire, you shall not be burned,*
> *nor will flames consume you.* (Isaiah 43:2)

Motivated by this court experience, I decided not to wait for something from my past to come to the surface again. I decided to take action myself. Especially since I was encouraged to do so by the Scripture, which I was becoming more and more familiar with. I had no doubts – I had to settle all my debts – this was God's will and I wanted to fulfill it.

I knew that somewhere in the files of the Hamburg Traffic Department there were unpaid fines for my 'free rides'. I decided to start there. During a visit to the *Hamburger Hochbahn* headquarters I was told that I owed 900 marks for fare evasion. I wrote a request to have this sum divided into installments of 50 marks per month. After a while, I received a positive answer. A definite date was also set for me to start paying my debt.

Trusting in God's help, I slowly began to settle all my 'overdue' obligations. These two matters were already under control, but that was not all. One more thing remained. I had to pay three months' rent for the apartment from which I had been evicted.

Suddenly I got financially out of breath as my expenses skyrocketed. I moved from my parish home to an independent apartment nearby. I needed some furniture. I was paying child support. On top of that, there was a rent to pay for the new apartment, the court-ordered fine, the unpaid fares installments. It all piled up. That's why I put off the settling of the unpaid rent until later.

Only a few years later did I return to it. When I had collected the necessary amount of money, I went to my old address, to the apartment from which I had been thrown out. In the office I met the facility manager, whom I knew well. I told him in a few words my story and what I had come with. The man said that he remembered me well and also remembered the circumstances under which we had parted. When I said that I came to settle the debt, he was

Chapter 5 A new beginning

very surprised. There were different people living in the building he managed. I was not the first one who had failed to pay the rent, but I was the first one who, years later, came to voluntarily settle the liability. I had to explain to him that I was only doing this because I wanted to obey God, who required me to do just that.

The manager said that unfortunately he was unable to help me. He was not entitled to take money from me because the house no longer belonged to the same landlord. The house had been sold and the only thing known about the previous owner was that he had moved out of Hamburg and there was no contact with him. In the end he said that he admired my decision, but I should keep the money for myself and consider the matter as settled.

Being homeless, I had been in hospital and a sobering-up facility several times. Without health insurance, every visit to such a place costs a lot of money. The bill might have grown really high, which made me thrill. The only thing I could do was to pray to God that He would help me to settle the debts. Everything seemed to indicate that my prayer was successful. Neither the hospital nor the sobering-up center filed any claims. Praised be the Lord!

Chapter 6

Growing in the spirit

> *May the God of peace himself make you perfectly holy and may you entirely, spirit, soul, and body, be preserved blameless for the coming of our Lord Jesus Christ.*

1 Thessalonians 5:23

SINCE I found my refuge in the parish house I noticed a tremendous change in the way I thought and behaved. Everything that used to occupy my mind, everything that I used to want to have and that was once of great importance to me, like money, luxurious things or traveling around the world, began to fade when faced with the experience of the close presence of Jesus Christ. I kept thinking about God. I was afraid to offend Him and lose Him. It got to the point where I stopped using an after-shave balm because I thought God might not like it. I just wanted to be with Him. To get to know Him. Everything else became irrelevant. After work, I would go back to my room, sit on my bed, pick up the Bible (a gift from Iwona) and read, read, read.

I was in a very handy situation. The church was near. Above me, Fr. Joachim von Stockchausen had his apartment. Upstairs was the chapel where we would gather every evening for a short prayer. Behind the wall was the apartment of the Rawalski family, who had lived in Hamburg for years and with whom we had prayer meetings once a week. I was surrounded on all sides by people of faith. I could watch them, listen to them and take my first steps in faith with them. I still had problems with the German language, so both Iwona and Dotothea Rawalska (Dorothea was a certified Polish-German translator) were eager to help me.

Father Joachim, Norbert and Ilse Friedrich, Peter Rawalski (Dorothea's husband), and Iwona Madziar, who was very patient with me, became my family. Everything I wanted to do and all my questions and doubts I consulted with them. Every day I thanked God for those people.

It was at that time that a priest from Poland, Father Leszek Irek, came to our parish. He became my first confessor and spiritual director. Even after he left for Poland, we kept in touch. He always helped me to understand the things that bothered me, helped to solve my problems, explained me about faith, the Church and the Holy Scriptures. From him I learned about the Light-Life Movement, of which Father Leszek Irek was a moderator. He spoke with such commitment about formation in the Light-Life Movement that I wanted very much to get involved in such a community. Once again Iwona, who had been associated with the movement before, came with help. The founder of the Movement, Father Franciszek Blachnicki[1] spent the last years of his life

---

[1] Franciszek Blachnicki (1921–1987) – Polish Catholic priest, university professor, prisoner of German Nazi concentration camps, persecuted under Poland's communist regime, charismatic organizer of Christian movements: Temperance Crusade, Light-Life (Oasis) Movement, Crusade for the Liberation of Man and Christian Service for the Liberation

Chapter 6 Growing in the spirit

in Germany and opened the Center of the Light-Life Movement in Carlsberg. It is about 600 kilometers away from Hamburg. I asked Iwona to take me there one day.

My language problems did not allow me to participate fully in the meetings. I tried to learn German as much as I could. I even went to a course. But the fruits of my labor were poor. Someone suggested that I get my hearing tested. I took a hearing test and it turned out that I couldn't hear some German sounds. Having listened to loud music through headphones when I was young, I could not hear German consonants at all. After several tests, the doctors concluded that I would always have problems learning the language. The only saving grace was a hearing aid.

I really wanted to join a Polish prayer group, but there was none in my area. Therefore, as soon as I heard about Carlsberg, some hope dawned on me. As I listened to Iwona's stories about this place I believed more and more that I could participate in the formation of my spiritual life of faith there.

Finally we went to Carlsberg. I had high hopes for this trip. And I was not disappointed. Carlsberg is a small village. It's about 50 km away from the bigger city, Mannheim. In this village there was the Polish Center of the Light-Life Movement, *Marianum*. The next few years of my life were connected with this place. I was delighted with the atmosphere at *Marianum*. Everyone was so joyful. We prayed together, we worked together. And everyone spoke Polish! It seemed to me as if I was in the most wonderful place in the world. There were wonderful priests and nuns. And the

---

of Nations. Founder of communities of consecrated life, such as the Institute of the Immaculate Mother of the Church, Community of Christ the Servant, and Union of Priests of Christ the Servant. Venerable Servant of God of the Catholic Church.

guests – seemingly unknown, but already so close to my heart.

Although everyone I met there showed me a great heart, it was Father Ireneusz Kopacz who was the most attentive to me, or so I felt at the time. He invited me to his room and asked me about my past, in a very gentle way. I had told him a little about myself. He asked me then if I would tell the whole story in the chapel during Mass the next day. I was totally surprised and unprepared for a things like that! I had never spoken to so many people before. I was terribly scared. I thought, 'What is this priest suggesting? Am I supposed to stand out there in front of the audience, take the microphone and talk about myself? I will surely burn with fear and embarrassment!' But at the same time, I somehow couldn't say 'no' to him! I said I would think about it and give an answer the next morning.

That night was a horror! Not even for a moment did I sleep a wink. The darkest scenarios kept appearing in my mind. I saw myself standing in front of people, all red and in sweat. Everyone was looking at me. How embarrassing! 'Even if I somehow manage to stay there for a while, what will I say?' The best solution in this situation would be to run away. But how? And where?

I remembered the words of a song once popular in Poland, *'Just get on a train...'* The problem was that the nearest train was leaving from Mannheim. I couldn't fight these thoughts. I got up and started praying. Once I hoped I would be able to fall asleep, I went back to bed, but sleep would not come. I started praying again. I struggled like this until morning. I was sure to see Father Ireneusz at breakfast. 'What will I tell him? I'll say that I can't, that I'm scared to death.'

I told Father Ireneusz that I had thought everything over and finally I said... 'I agree!'. There were maybe fifteen

Chapter 6 Growing in the spirit

people having breakfast in the canteen. And I had already met everyone the previous day, so I decided that saying something to this handful of people wouldn't be a big deal. The Mass was beginning at noon, so I still had some time to arrange my thoughts. I walked around the premises. An hour before the Mass I noticed that something unexpected was going on. There were more and more cars coming to the parking lot. More and more people were arriving to *Marianum*. 'What is the meaning of this?' Somewhere in the hall I caught up with Iwona and asked her who all these people were. She answered that Poles from nearby villages and towns always come to Carlsberg for the Sunday Mass. Finally the chapel was packed with people silently waiting for the Mass to begin. The chapel was filled to the brim! And I was supposed to go out and tell all these people about myself! 'Father Ireneusz! What have you done to me?!'

I hoped the Mass would be postponed, or something. However, at noon, the Eucharist began. Because of my performance I was sitting in the first pew and could not see what was going on behind me, but subconsciously I could feel the breaths of the people who in a moment would surely criticize my performance. I felt really bad.

When the time came, Father Ireneusz called me to the pulpit. When I got to the microphone and looked around, I thought I would faint. So many people! Everyone was looking at me. Everyone was expecting something. What could I tell them, an uneducated man like me, who actually could not speak? What could I give them? So I began to talk just to avoid fainting. I was afraid of looking them in the eyes, so I looked at the ceiling or in front of me and told them who I was, when and how I heard about Jesus, and how I got free from addictions.

I had agreed with Father Ireneusz that it would be a very short testimony, five to seven minutes. In reality I spoke for over half an hour. Did I talk so long because I had something to talk about? No, I just didn't know how to finish! I didn't know when my seven minutes were up. But when I finished, I heard thunderous applause.

For the first time in my life I heard applause during the Mass. And it was for me! As soon as the Mass was over, the people just rushed at me. Some thanked me for what I had said, others congratulated me and told their stories. 'What is going on?' I thought. 'Didn't they all see that I almost died of fear at the pulpit?'

After dinner we all left *Marianum*. I had a joyful but also scary experience of my first stay in Carlsberg. But I knew I would be there again. We were to come back to *Marianum* once a month.

A month later I was driving there on my own. I had to be there. They all spoke my native language. There was such a wonderful atmosphere there. It was a place for me. I could stay there forever if it weren't for my job. I was hoping that this time Father Ireneusz would leave me alone. Everyone had already heard my testimony a month before. During this stay, I would only take care of myself. It was supposed to be relaxed, without stress. But Father Ireneusz had other plans. He had just started a formation in accordance with the program of the Light-Life Movement, entitled 'Ten steps towards Christian maturity.' I wanted to grow, I wanted to grow spiritually and this kind of formation satisfied my desire to know more. I decided to come here every month and go through all the formation steps. But there was one more 'surprise' waiting for me. Father Ireneusz decided that I would lead one of the small formation groups.

Chapter 6 Growing in the spirit

'What does he want from me?' I thought with anger. I had never led a group of people in my life. I always wanted to belong, but I wanted to be led, not to lead! I knew I was no leader. Unfortunately, just like before, I couldn't refuse the priest.

Again the same fear. Again I wanted to run away. My only consolation was that each participant had a script with topics for a specific step. This thought gave me some comfort. I planned to begin the meeting with the 'Our Father' prayer and say something else at the end. Let the others speak during the meeting. After all, this was supposed to be sharing. I would be the host only. However, my cunning plan failed. Every once in a while someone would ask me a question that I would have to answer. At that time, I learned about 'praying in the spirit,' and while others were saying something, I used my break to pray for support. Somehow I made it through! Despite the difficulties, I was very happy with the trip. The next step was to be accomplished in a month.

When I arrived there the next time, I was surprised by something really interesting. On the previous meeting there was an architect in my group, if I remember correctly his name was Grzegorz. He came with a friend, Marian. When they were driving to Carlsberg for a meeting, Grzegorz, a real chatterbox, was talking all the time time. After the meeting, however, on the way back home something happened to Grzegorz – he didn't say anything for a long part of the journey. Finally Marian asked him why he was silent. Grzegorz answered briefly, 'I'm thinking about what Heniek said.'

Grzegorz admitted that when he had learned that he would be in my group, he was not happy. He grew in a family of strong believers and had been learning about Scripture since childhood. And he found out he was going to be in a formation group led by a recently converted alcoholic. An alcoholic was to tell him about the Word of God? If not disappointed, he was skeptical. What I had said a month before, however, touched him so much that he absolutely wanted to meet with me again and stay in my group.

I did not get it at all. After our small group meeting I was convinced I was a miserable failure. I said something because I had to say something, but in my opinion it was all without order and composition, without any value. Meanwhile, Grzegorz heard something different. Did we attend the same meeting? Or was he listening to someone else? While I was thinking about it, I remembered what Father Ireneusz had said before the meeting. Responding to my lamentation that I didn't know what to say, he said that it was not me, but the Holy Spirit who would lead the meeting, and He would also speak. I think he was right. Grzegorz didn't listen to me, he listened to the Holy Spirit.

I attended the 'Ten Steps to Christian Maturity' every month. In between I worked on the matter at home, preparing intensely for the subsequent meetings.

Although I still felt fear, I was no longer so reluctant to lead a small group. It was fun after all! Then, all of a sudden, the crazy priest Ireneusz came up with a new idea. He created the 'Diakonia of Evangelization', which I joined, of course. The task of the Diakonia was not only to hold meetings in the *Marianum* Centre, but first of all, to go out into the world with the Word of God. We went from home to home, from door to door. We did evangelistic actions in front of supermarkets. We were looking for Polish communities. We visited cities, towns and villages. We organized meetings. Whenever there was an opportunity to preach the Word, Father Ireneusz did not let go. He would pack us in his

Chapter 6 Growing in the spirit

car and we set off to proclaim Jesus Christ, whether it was *'convenient or inconvenient.'*[2]

The other day, the priest suggested that we go to a gas station on the *Autobahn* at dawn. There was a huge parking lot for trucks by the gas station. Polish drivers were staying there overnight. I didn't like that idea because of the time we were to do it. Walking around the parking lot at dawn with a guitar and waking up tired drivers? I gently shared my doubts with the priest. I wished I could somehow stop him. I had a strong argument, 'We must not interrupt the drivers' sleep. Let's wait until they wake up on their own.' Then Father Ireneusz countered, 'If we don't wake them up, they will wake up on their own and drive away. Who will tell them about Jesus then?' Unyielding, as always!

This way, God – using other people, especially Father Ireneusz – was forming my new character. He was freeing me from fear in dealing with people. He was forming a new attitude in me. He taught me a new language. He set new goals.

My spiritual growth was not just about Carlsberg. I worked on it in my everyday life. I wanted to be a disciple of Jesus. Even then I understood that the title of disciple belongs to those who learn. I decided to learn something every day. The formation obtained in the Light-Life Movement seemingly wasn't enough for me, so I enrolled in the Correspondence Bible Course run by the Jesuits from Cracow. My fascination with the Holy Scriptures grew. In the Book of Amos (8:11) we read:

> *See, days are coming—oracle of the Lord God—*
> *when I will send a famine upon the land:*

---

[2]Compare: 2 Timothy 4:2

Henryk Krzosek 🕊 GOD FOUND ME ON THE STREET

Not a hunger for bread, or a thirst for water,
but for hearing the word of the Lord.

How much the words of this prophecy fit me. My days of hungering for bread and thirsting for drink were over. Now there was a hunger to hear what God has to say. So more and more books appeared in my apartment, especially Bible commentaries. I adopted a rule: I would not sleep unless I learned something, read something. In one of the books I read and remembered a sentence that became the motto of my life: 'If a Christian experiences two days at the same spiritual level, he fails.'

I wanted to learn. I wanted to pray. But I also wanted to share my joy with others. That was something I still lacked. I was still in the German 'Nathanael' community. Although Dorothea, Peter and Iwona spoke Polish, the meetings were held in German. I wanted Carlsberg in Hamburg. Iwona sometimes spoke of wanting to create and lead a Polish group, but her commitment to the German Church and the studies she was still attending did not make it possible to take on additional responsibilities. Our conversations about this ended with the statement: we need to pray for a Polish-speaking group. So I prayed, prayed, prayed.

Suddenly I realized that it was time to act. I called Iwona. When we met, I explained that I was convinced and we had to do something about it. But what? We considered various options of how and whom to invite to participate. Maybe someone we know? Maybe we should talk to someone? Nothing was coming together.

The great hope in all this was the fact that there was a Polish Mass in our parish of St. Wilhelm once a month and many Poles came. Maybe we could start here? The pastor, Fr. Joachim helped us with everything. He soon invited me to

Chapter 6 Growing in the spirit

his office and said, 'Henryk, it can't go on like this. I have Polish weddings on Saturdays and Polish baptisms on Sundays, a lot of Poles live in the neighborhood, and we don't have any Polish formation group. We have to do something about it.' I replied that I had already talked about this with Iwona, but we didn't know how to begin. Fr. Joachim promised that he would talk to the Polish priest who was coming to celebrate the Mass next Sunday and that he would announce after Mass that there would be the first meeting of the Polish prayer group in the parish hall. 'Everyone interested is welcome.'

On that Sunday about forty people came to the hall after the Mass. I don't know what was their motivation – probably sheer curiosity. When Iwona explained that we wanted to start a Polish prayer group, which would be meeting once a week in my new apartment, six people from the whole group declared they would come to the first meeting. We planned it for the following Thursday.

From Sunday to Thursday, I thought about nothing else but this meeting. I didn't worry too much because Iwona was responsible for everything. I was only supposed to make the apartment available and prepare coffee and tea. But I really wanted the meeting to go well, so I prayed and asked others to pray for this intention. I called Fr. Ireneusz because in Carlsberg there was an ongoing intercessory prayer for various intentions. We needed their support. And we received it...

On Thursday Iwona and I were waiting for our first guest. Punctually at 6 p.m. someone rang the doorbell. Our hearts jumped. When I opened the door I saw four unknown people. Someone asked if prayer meetings were to be held here. I confirmed and invited them inside. After a short introduction, it turned out that they were two married couples: Marysia and Piotr Jankowski (Piotr is the drummer of the band *NEW LIFE'm*) and Justyna and Bogdan Rytlewski. We served them some tea and some cake and, while waiting for the others, we started to get to know each other. Iwona asked how they found out about our meeting (they were not in the parish hall on Sunday). The first surprise: all four of them lived in Hamburg and they found out about the meeting in Sankt Augustin, a city about 450 kilometers from Hamburg. They had come to a retreat for married couples there and someone suggested them to attend our meeting, giving my address. No one else came that day. Iwona did her best and we were all happy. We decided to meet next week.

Another meeting and another surprise: the first doorbell rang and again some strangers asked if it was the place where prayer meetings were held. As it turned out, they were students from Cracow who came to Hamburg for an internship. They found out about the meeting and the address before they left Cracow.

A moment later, Marysia with Piotr and Justyna with Bogdan joined us. It got pretty crowded. There was no furniture in the one-room apartment I had just rented. All I had was a mattress, a desk and two chairs and we still could hardly fit in. Although it was cramped and uncomfortable because most of us were sitting against the walls on the floor, we joyfully worshiped God and felt His presence. We all wanted to keep meeting. We also wanted to invite others. In this situation we concluded that my apartment was too small. Marysia and Piotr proposed that we move to their place.

Soon the apartment of the Jankowskis was also too small for us. God kept sending new people. We were growing fast. Then Iwona suggested that she would talk to the Fr. Joachim so that our group could meet in the parish hall. In this way

Chapter 6 Growing in the spirit

the meetings of the Polish prayer group began to take place in the German parish of St. Wilhelm in Hamburg.

I was very happy. From meeting to meeting there were more and more of us. Iwona played the guitar, prepared short catechesis and everything was in Polish. One day Iwona announced that she was leaving for two weeks for evangelization. To Siberia. How nice! And who would lead the meetings? I knew what to expect. Iwona wanted me to lead the meetings. There was no turning back. I had to agree. I already had some experience from Carlsberg, some notes. It was only two meetings. In the end it was six, because Iwona returned to Hamburg much later than she had planned.

It got to the point where we had about 40 people coming to the Thursday meetings. We proposed that all participants go once a month to Carlsberg for further formation. We used different means of transportation. Sometimes it was a private car, other times a train, and even when there was a larger group, Piotr Jankowski borrowed a minibus from the pastor of the Polish Catholic Mission.

This is how our formation adventure with the Light-Life Movement began. When the German part of the 'Nathanael' community saw us flourish and the enthusiasm we had for the monthly visits in Carlsberg, they decided to check what was going on. Several people with their leaders Norbert and Ilse Friedrich went with us to Carlsberg. Our brothers and sisters from 'Nathanael' liked the atmosphere of the center but above all the vision of a continuous and structured formation. They also decided to join the Light-Life Movement to start formation among Germans in Hamburg.

We were growing both spiritually and in number. I think that the time was good for us. Not only in Germany, not only in Poland, but in the whole of Europe we could feel a certain movement of the Holy Spirit. Probably in response to this movement, leaders of various churches organized the International Conference of Leaders of the Holy Spirit Renewal in Brno, Switzerland. At the urging of Iwona and Norbert I went there with 'Nathanael'. I decided to go also because I knew that I would meet many of my friends from Carlsberg, especially the 'crazy' Father Ireneusz Kopacz and Father Jan Kruczyński, whom I had also met in Carsberg.

On the second day of the Conference during the morning common prayer, something happened to me. Earlier I had heard a lot about the fire of the Holy Spirit. I knew the Gospel announcement of John the Baptist who said that Jesus Christ would 'baptize you with the Holy Spirit and with fire' (Matthew 3:11), but I still didn't know what those words meant. 'What is this fire?'

That morning everything was about to become clear. The prayer began. Everyone prayed loudly and simultaneously, in different languages. One big noise. It seemed to me that this great noise was about to blow the roof off. I was in the middle of this prayer. What was this mighty power? It took possession of me. I felt like I was being pulled out of deep water. I was emerging into something different, something new, something that was just beginning. And this fire in my heart. My heart was on fire! I could feel it! That fire was burning so beautifully in me that I started jumping up and down for joy. My hands went up in worship. I didn't want it to end. Although the prayer ended after a while, the conviction that I was entering into something new remained.

I did not understand it. My experience was accompanied by a strong desire for confession. I could not find Father Ireneusz anywhere to confess and ask what was happening to me. Where is he? I have such an experience and he is not there!

Chapter 6 Growing in the spirit

The next day, right after breakfast, still unable to find Father Ireneusz, I went to confession to another priest. He listened to me attentively and said that the promise of the Father, which Jesus spoke about, had been fulfilled on me during the prayer. I was baptized with the Holy Spirit and fire.

Crisis of faith

> *Why are you confused and why is doubt stirring in your hearts?*
>
> Luke 24:38

Days passed. Months passed. I grew higher and higher in my spiritual life. It was all beautiful. What I didn't understand was why most of the people I met didn't take advantage of it. I wanted so much to talk about the love of God and the goodness of Jesus Christ, but whenever I spoke, they were not interested. Most of all, I didn't understand my friends still living homeless on the streets. 'Why don't they want what I have got?'

And when I was rescued from my homelessness, God gave me home with a priest who had invited Mother Teresa of Calcutta three months before my conversion. Fr. Joachim invited her because he had obtained a house and he wanted to use it as a food center for the homeless. He wanted Sisters of Mother Teresa to run the facility. Mother Teresa came, looked at the house and agreed to send sisters to work there. All she asked was that the pastor build a chapel.

Less than three months later, the soup kitchen with the sisters was up and running, and during that time, being a new convert, I found my home in the parish. The pastor skillfully took advantage of me staying in his parish and my skills. He suggested that I assist in the construction of the chapel, if possible. This made me get in touch with my homeless friends whom I had left quite recently, and who began to visit the new soup kitchen.

At first I was somehow uncomfortable. I disappeared from the street suddenly and now I was there in the facility run by nuns. My friends from the previous soup kitchens, mostly Poles, surprised by my transformation, asked me, 'What happened to you?' A little awkwardly I tried to explain where it all had come from. But when I pointed to God as the perpetrator, they would shake their heads and, with a grin on their faces, they would immediately move on to another topic.

But most often, when we talked like this and I had a chance to talk a bit longer, I heard, 'You've made it.' 'You're lucky.' 'You are strong.' 'You have good fate.' Why didn't they all believe that it was God who gave me freedom? I couldn't deal with it. After all, they all know me and know who I was not so long ago. I thought, 'I've had many bottles of vodka with them. And now when they hear that God changed my whole life, they just think I've gone bonkers.'

One of the sisters who took care of the soup kitchen came from Poland. Because of a lot of Poles came to the *Haus Betlehem* (that's how the soup kitchen was called), the Sister decided to organize meetings with an additional meal for them. Knowing my past, she invited me as well. I couldn't wait for the first meeting. I thought that when I had Sister's support everyone would believe that it was God who had set me free. And they would all come to Jesus and get what I got. In my imagination I was seeing those conversions!

Chapter 6 Growing in the spirit

With this attitude, I came to the first meeting. It is easy to guess how my former buddies reacted. A heated discussion ensued, and the most difficult questions were asked, one by one, 'If God exists, then why this and why that?' I went home furious. Where was this God who told me to tell everyone how He had taken pity on me and what He had done to me? After all, that passage from the Gospel of Mark, 'Go home to your own people and tell them what the Lord has done for you, and how he has had mercy on you.' (5:19), was for me, I was more than convinced of that. 'I did return to my own people and told them what the Lord had done for me, but they laughed. Why?' Another meeting, and another, and still nothing came out of my plans.

Doubts were growing. 'Maybe it was really some kind of fate and not God? Maybe I had some kind of luck? Or maybe I somehow, out of my consciousness, revived my inner strength and stopped drinking? After all, everything can be explained more rationally.' My first spiritual awe began to wane. I no longer felt God's presence so much. I no longer felt so confident. There were more and more questions instead of signs from God.

By this time I had become familiar with the entire liturgical year in the Church, and when I learned that now there would only be repetitions: year A, year B, and year C... out of a sudden I felt disappointed. 'Lord, is this all the Church can offer me. Just repetitions? If so – I say: no, thank you.'

I felt the need for something more. The fire that was ignited in me in Switzerland was still burning. I went through formation in the Light-Life Movement. I formed at home. I studied. I read many books. I learned the whole Small Catechism (the new one was published only in 1994). I prayed the breviary prayer. I attended meetings. I even was myself a leader. And what? All I had now there doubts, doubts, doubts!

Full of anxiety I went to the Polish Catholic Mission in Hamburg. I wanted to visit a bookstore, believing that I would find some comfort there. 'God, I am looking for You. Where are you? What's next for me?' As I was browsing, my gaze stopped on a small red book lying on a table. It had a foreign-language title, completely incomprehensible to me. I moved on to other items. As I browsed through the various books, I somehow kept returning with my thoughts to the one with the foreign title. 'What is this?' I went back to that table and picked up the red book. I read on the cover: John Paul II, *'Christifideles laici'*. The title didn't tell me anything, but I looked inside and there it read: *'On the Vocation and Mission of the Lay Faithful in the Church and the World.'* I quickly flipped through the book. I read a few sentences and then went to the table of contents. I was becoming convinced that what I was holding in my hand might be what I was looking for. I went to the checkout and after a while I was in possession of a mysterious red book with a Latin title that meant nothing to me yet.

I wanted to quickly read what was inside. I went to the bank of the Elba, sat down on a bench and started reading. What I read slowly began to work in me. The doubts I had been harboring up to that point were melting away. A different and completely new face of the Church was emerging for me, as if out of dense fog. A Church that calls me not only to participate in the liturgy, but also to work. A Church that cries out: 'It is not fair to stay idle!'

As I continued to read, tears began to stream from my eyes. I heard God's voice more and more clearly, *'You too*

Chapter 6 Growing in the spirit

go into my vineyard'.[3] 'No matter how old I am. How much time I have wasted standing idle. Now God is calling me to work in His vineyard, which is the Church and... the whole world.' Weeping, I got up from the bench and walked around still reading. I walked back and forth and then sat down again. I couldn't take my eyes off what I was reading. God was laying out before me a wonderful future of cooperation. I understood what I was to fill my life with, and if I went in that direction, it could not be boring. Jesus promised that He would give us life in abundance. I was just now learning what it should look like from John Paul II's Exhortation *'ON THE VOCATION AND THE MISSION OF THE LAY FAITHFUL IN THE CHURCH AND IN THE WORLD.'*

In the evening, after reading the entire Exhortation, I returned home tired. As if I hadn't had enough reading, I reached for the Bible. I opened it at random and read the now familiar phrase spoken by John the Baptist, the words: *'He will baptize you with the Holy Spirit and fire.'*[4] How amazing. Not so long ago, in Switzerland, God had lit that fire in me. It kept on burning. I kept wanting to know God. To help people. To get involved in the Church. And on the other hand, I had more and more doubts, 'Does all this make any sense?' I expected beautiful fruits, that I would do something valuable for God, but only frustration came.

Today I know that faith will always be a struggle. This is inherent in the spiritual life of every believer. The adversary of God and man, the devil, will do anything to discourage us and push us off the path we have chosen. I have just learned my first lesson, which was to make me realize that life with God is not always sweet candy, but may sometimes also be

---

[3] Matthew 20:7
[4] Matthew 3:11

bitter. In this battle of ours, one thing is certain: God does not take the adversity away, but finally He always wins!

> *No trial has come to you but what is human. God is faithful and will not let you be tried beyond your strength; but with the trial he will also provide a way out, so that you may be able to bear it.* (1 Corinthians 10:13)

Isn't that beautiful? God will never allow me to be tempted beyond what I can overcome. No such doubts will ever come that will be able to push me into darkness. God will always show me the way out. The only thing for me to do is to seek God's guidance. I found it in John Paul II's exhortation *'Christifideles laici'*. I survived and became stronger. Praise the Lord!

No matter how many years had to pass before I understood that it is not *I* who does something for God, but it is *God* who does something in me. When I am reading today the words of St. Paul written in the Letter to the Philippians (2:13), *'For God is the one who, for his good purpose, works in you both to desire and to work'*, I eventually understand why I then went to the Polish Catholic Mission Bookstore, why I paid attention to the red book on the table, why I bought it, why I started to read it. It was not me who invented it, but God who became the cause of my wanting and acting. He was the one who came up with the idea that this would be the way to answer my doubts and show me the way out. He put this desire and action in my heart. Why? Because He loves me and will never leave me!

Chapter 7

Real signs

> *Look! I am for you! I will turn my face toward you; you will be plowed and planted. Upon you I will multiply the whole house of Israel...*
>
> Ezekiel 36:9–10a

I WAS learning a new life. I was slowly coming to grips with the fact that life with God is not all sunny days, but that there are also faith shortages and various difficulties that one would like to avoid. As I studied the Scriptures each day I came across more and more verses that spoke of trials and tests. These conflicted with my previous experience of God's love, goodness, and care. I tried to push it aside, but it kept coming back and making me think. Today I know that God wanted me to work through something which was in me.

In the Letter to the Hebrews (12:6) we read, *'for whom the Lord loves, he disciplines; he scourges every son he acknowledges.'* These words terrified me! I knew my condition. I wanted to be better and more pleasing to God, but I was not always successful. Why would the loving God–Father take it out on me?

Luckily I found another verse a while later, in the Letter of James (1:2–3), *'Consider it all joy, my brothers, when you encounter various trials, for you know that the testing of your faith produces perseverance.'* This calmed me down a bit. I began to understand that through trials God was forming a new person in me. I received a deeper understanding of what I was facing by meditating the words that form the motto of this chapter, *'you will be plowed and planted'*.

Prophet Ezekiel shows us the way God does things. If a farmer wants to collect rich harvest, he must first properly prepare the field. So our Lord prepares us through various trials so that the harvest will be abundant. Preparing the ground for sowing is not pleasant, but it must be done if we are to expect the fruit. In the same way, we as believers should without hesitation submit to God's 'plowing' so that we can bring others to Jesus Christ. I began to realize that there is a time in the life of a Christian when God sets him aside – to a spiritual desert. Such examples are described in the Bible. Before Moses became the leader of the people he had to 'work through' himself in the desert. John the Baptist also wandered across the desert until he was thirty years old. During that time he did not utter a word, he did not baptize a single man. Was he not able to do this? He was, but he had to wait for his time. Even Jesus himself lived hidden in his parents' house until He came across John the Baptist. And what happened to St. Paul immediately after his conversion at Damascus? His zeal to preach the risen Jesus was so great that people wanted to kill him. What did God do? He sent him to his hometown and hid him in the desolation for several years.

With this bit of wisdom already in place, I was able to look back into my not-too-distant past and understand my failures in the field of evangelism. My heart was on fire, but

Chapter 7 Real signs

it was not yet that time. However, once God had 'plowed through' me a bit, I was able to see some fruit, and that gave me encouragement to be even more submissive to God.

Our whole prayer group met for some time at the house of Marysia and Piotr Jankowski. One of Marysia's brothers, Józek[1], was struggling with a problem which I also had not been able to cope with until recently – alcoholism. We all wondered how we could help Józek. He lived in Paris and Marysia had only sporadic phone contact with him. Due to the fact that Józek and Piotr had not only family- but also professional ties (Józek was crafting jewelry and Piotr was selling it) the Jankowskis decided to invite Józek to Hamburg, ostensibly for professional reasons, but mainly so that Józek could meet me and hear about my transformation. So it happened. What resulted from it? Józek will tell about it himself. He has sent me his testimony.

My short testimony

> My name is Józef Żelazny. I was born in Gdańsk, Poland, in 1953. I spent most of my life this city and its neighborhood. I come from a family with a strong catholic background. I am the second of twelve siblings. I was an altar boy all through elementary school, so close to the Church, and I remember feeling good there. In my teenage years I walked away from God. When I was 18, I got drunk; so began my boozy life, which smoothly turned into hard alcoholism. To illustrate what it looked like: in 1975, when I was 22, I was sitting to my final high school exam in the Polish language. I couldn't concentrate, so I went to the restroom, drank some vodka from a pocket flask, came back and finished my

---
[1] A diminutive form of *Józef* (Joseph). See footnote on page 84.

essay. I passed the exam with flying colors! For the next 20 years I was constantly drunk, with varying intensity.

God had blessed me with various talents and abilities, good things kept happening to me, someone would say I was a lucky guy. But I was going downhill, which at first was invisible to those around me, but with time the truth came out. I got married quickly, and soon my wife ran away from me. I entered into new relationships hurting others and myself. The years 1990–1991 were the climax of my alcoholic degeneration, I wasn't homeless yet, but I knew it was a matter of time – short time.

I actually met Henio[2] Krzosek in the spring of 1991, when we were driving with Marysia and Piotr Jankowski from Hamburg to Essen for a day pilgrimage. I went with them to this 'event' rather out of politeness for the Jankowskis, with whom I had been staying for a few weeks, taking care of my otherwise murky business. In the evening we arrived in the town of Marl. There was a planned evangelistic service taking place there, in which I rather didn't participate, I just wandered around the church or the area. But at some point I entered this hall (chapel) and I saw that this Heniu, who had been traveling with me for a couple of hours, was now standing and speaking to the crowd of people. And that's what I heard, 'I was an alcoholic, I was homeless for two years, I was roaming on *St. Pauli*' etc. And then I thought to myself, 'How is this Heniu not ashamed to say such things about himself in public in the church?'

But from that moment on, the thought also began to haunt me, '**If he came out of such a pit and has been clean for two years now, maybe something like that could happen to me, too?**' I think Henio's

---

[2]*Henio* (or *Heniu*) is another diminutive form of the name Henryk, usually used by an adult person towards a preteen boy. If used to address an adult, the form *Henio* expresses a deeper, friendly affection and loving respect. See footnote on page 84.

Chapter 7 Real signs

testimony directly contributed to my conversion. Something happened at that time. Going on a pilgrimage from Hamburg, I took a huge bottle of wine in my bag for the road – I brought it back intact. Yes, there was another deep alcoholic fall. I almost ended up in prison because of my swindles, which 'accidentally' came to light. In the end, a few weeks later I went to an *Oasis* in Krościenko[3]. The First Degree formation lasted two weeks. I lived in a room with Henio and Fr Ireneusz Kopacz. I remember that I watched Henio and others very closely to see if there was any pretending, games etc. But it was there that the decision was made: to accept Jesus as the Lord. God really came into my life when I asked Him to. **After 20 years of heavy drinking I was healed from alcoholism**.

I went back to Gdańsk and waited to see what would happen. I woke up every morning without a hangover, and most importantly, after many years I started to live a sacramental life. In the morning, instead of drinking the usual 'hair of the dog', I was receiving Holy Communion, with really great joy. This continued for 20 years. I didn't undergo any specialized post-alcoholic therapy, my therapy was being in the community of the Light-Life Movement, full formation, and then forming others. Jesus gave me the grace to evangelize also in Eastern Europe. In 1992–1997 I was in Belarus every month helping to lead [the formation course] *STEPS TO CHRISTIAN MATURITY*. If the Lord has worked something through me, praise Him for it. I keep on praying and I want to be a useful tool in His hand.

God is working, He is willing to use people who want to serve Him. I will probably never forget my embarrassment back then, when I was standing at the back of the church in Marl and listened to Henio's testimony.

---

[3] A picturesque village in southern Poland, in the Pieniny Mountains. A popular holiday destination.

> On the basis of his testimony of conversion, a desire for liberation, for freedom from addiction, was stirred within me. The next day Fr Ireneusz evangelised me on the way to Newiges, a few weeks later, at the end of the *Oasis* in Krościenko, Fr Jan Kruczyński gave me some valuable advice, and then for many years Fr Ireneusz Kopacz formed me. This is the Church.
>
> Józef Żelazny
>
> Oasis Community 'Precious Pearl' Mt 13:46
>
> Pruszcz Gdański, 16 June 2013

When I saw Józek's transformation, my doubts began to melt like snow in the sun. I finally accepted the thought that good God changed me by taking me in His hands and that He wanted me to help others to get rid of addictions by giving testimony about me being set free by Him. This conviction was accompanied by a growing love, patience and mercy for people who were enslaved and lost.

Although my first efforts to reach out to my friends from the street did not bring any results – apart from the growing discouragement – something started to improve when I met Józek and witnessed his transformation. I wanted to help them, although I didn't know how and where. So I began asking God to put such people on my path or to send me to them. The answer to my prayer came soon. Marysia Jankowska had a female friend from Poland, who lived in the neighborhood. Her brother, Romek Roślik, was a friend of Józek Żelazny's brother. Romek, who also ended up in Hamburg, had huge problems with alcohol.

Motivated by the amazing transformation of Józek, Marysia and Piotr Jankowski, together with Asia and Piotr Antczak (Asia is Marysia's childhood friend) decided to cast their nets on Romek. They suggested that Piotr and I should visit

Chapter 7 Real signs

Romek, who lived temporarily on a ship converted into accommodation for people applying for the right of residence in Germany. When we arrived we found him in bed, drunk of course. He opened his eyes, looked at us recognizing Piotr Jankowski and muttered, 'What a pig I am. I got drunk again' and that was all we saw of him. He simply ran away.

After some time we met again. This time in way better conditions for conversation – at the Jankowskis' house. I told Romek about my turbulent life and how I found freedom in Jesus Christ. To support my words that Jesus Christ is able to set him free from alcohol, we used a powerful argument, which was the change of Józek Żelazny. Since then Romek began appearing at our prayer meetings. There were even rumors that Romek was coming because he liked our animator and my spiritual director – Iwona. But this was not important. I have no idea what Romek's attitude was, but the most important thing is that once in the church he asked for a prayer for freedom from alcohol. Romek entrusted his life to Jesus, and Jesus gave him freedom.

There were already three of us. Józek, Romek and me. Not so long ago we were all immersed in alcohol, but now we were completely free, without any medical therapy. Jesus Christ simply became our therapist. We couldn't keep this supernatural grace only for ourselves. We got involved in the evangelization work led by Father Ireneusz Kopacz and the Light-Life Movement. I had to stay in Hamburg because of my work, while Józek and Romek joined Father Ireneusz and travelled with him along the paths of evangelisation not only in Germany but also in Europe and Asia, everywhere showing with their lives that true freedom is possible only in Jesus Christ, the Son of God.

Henryk Krzosek GOD FOUND ME ON THE STREET

In the summer of 1993 Father Ireneusz and I went to the Third Degree Oasis in Rome. Apart from the formation we also did street evangelism. We tried to reach all the places where we could find lost Poles, among others at the *Caritas* facility. During one such outing we came across a group of our mostly homeless compatriots. They were cleaning windows of cars that stopped at red lights. In this way they earned money not only to survive, but also to buy alcohol and drugs. In the group of men was Krzysiek Maćko, who at that time used to say that there are only two things that he never says: a prayer and 'no' to alcohol. I told him what Jesus had done in my life. Józek added something from himself.

Krzysiek decided to reconcile with God and entrust Him with his fate. Seeing his desire to change, Fr. Ireneusz took him to Carlsberg. After one year I got unexpectedly an invitation to Pelpin in Poland for a wedding. Krzysiek, already free from addictions, and Bożena, a participant of our Oasis in Rome, decided to get married and to testify together that nothing is impossible for God. The wedding was also supposed to demonstrate their freedom in Christ, that's why they decided to have it without alcohol. It was so joyful and boisterous that the late Bishop Jan Bernard Szlaga himself invited us for refreshments the next day.

It was the second consecutive alcohol-free wedding which I had attended. The first one took place some time before, in Carlsberg, where Romek Roślik married a beautiful Monika. There were more other weddings to come. Isn't that wonderful?

Years passed by. My desire to help enslaved people never faded. I worked hard on myself so that the grace I had received from Jesus Christ would not be wasted. All the

Chapter 7 Real signs

time I met people I could tell about the freedom God had given me. God never changes, and what He has done for my friends, He continues to do. Let me mention two more testimonies.

It was 2007 and I had been living and working again in Poland, in Szczecin, for over a year. I was a member of the 'Koinonia John the Baptist' community. Unexpectedly I got phone call from Gdynia. The unknown caller introduced himself as Grzegorz. He briefly explained what it was about – he was an alcoholic and he got my number from a psychologist. His wife recorded on video how he behaves when drunk. When he sobered up the next day, he watched the video and his drunken behavior and was horrified. He decided to seek help. Some kind of therapy. That's how he ended up with a psychologist who happened to be my sister from the Gdynia community of 'Koinonia John the Baptist', Małgosia Kornacka. Knowing my experience, Małgosia referred Grzegorz to me. I proposed a meeting. And so I went to Gdynia.

At the appointed time I appeared in Grzegorz's apartment. I listened to him and proposed praying together. He agreed. We prayed that God would change his life. After the prayer I suggested that we go together to a meeting of the community to recharge ourselves. That day Grzegorz was born to a new, alcohol-free life. I came back to Szczecin, and Grzegorz started his new adventure with Jesus Christ.

The next phone call from Grzegorz was about an invitation to a wedding with – needless to say – an alcohol-free party! Grzegorz had been in a civil union with Joasia for several years and they had a daughter. They had not had a sacramental marriage. Now they decided to do it. Several years have already passed. Today Grzegorz looks indifferently at the bottles of alcohol, which once wreaked so much havoc in his life.

Later on I moved back to Germany, to a small village located 10 km from the Polish border. The area where my village was located was much depopulated, just like many other locations of the former GDR. Many young people had moved to western Germany in search of work or a better living. They had left their homes, so the German government offered apartments, houses or even whole farms at low prices to newcomers from Poland. In this way, new Polish families move in from time to time. I found a small flat in an apartment building.

Soon a couple with a child moved into the building where I lived. Watching my new neighbor through the window, I saw tattoos nearly all over his body. I thought he must have had an interesting past. I wanted to talk to him. To start a conversation I rolled up my shirt sleeves to show him that I also had tattoos. I thought it would make it easier to strike up a conversation. I grabbed a bag of garbage and walked outside the building. It worked. My goal was obvious – to tell about Jesus Christ. During the first conversation, I told my neighbor who I was and how Jesus came into my life. Then Marcin (that was his name) said that he had the same problem that I once had. He was at that time on a rehab injection, but he was afraid that once the injection wore off, he would go back to drinking again. The injection was the second in a row, so the first one did not prevent him from getting back to drinking. 'Can this be changed?' He asked. I suggested a meeting at my home to discuss the issue. After a few days, we had a cup of coffee together.

My tactic has been the same for years. First I introduce my situation, which is who I was, what I was doing, and what I had gotten myself into. Then I briefly describe my encounter

Chapter 7 Real signs

with the living God in the person of Jesus Christ and the consequences of that encounter. Later, if my interlocutor wants, I propose to pray together.

Martin came with his wife and son. In the meantime I noticed that Jola was a heavy smoker. After I told her about myself and listened to what Jola and Marcin had to say, I proposed that we pray together. We asked God to come to Marcin and give him complete freedom from addictions. During the prayer I remembered that Jola also had a problem with cigarettes, so I prayed for her too. A few days later, I met Jola smiling and asking, 'Henryk, what have you done to me? I didn't want to quit smoking at all, and now I can't smoke!' I could only escape to God and explain that if something like that happened, I'm not the one who caused it, but God.

Marcin and Jola were born into a new life. The action of the rehab injection ceased, yet Marcin didn't feel any desire to drink. Jola is happy that she no longer has to spend so much money on cigarettes.

Is their life all sorted out and settled? No. Only now, when they have accepted Jesus as their Lord and Savior, does He help them to put everything in order. Not so long ago, Marcin was not even baptized, but today he is a new member of the Church. Living far from God, they didn't care much about living a sacramental life. Today they know how much they needed to be sacramentally bound to each other – forever.

We lived in the same village, in the same building, in the same staircase and on the same floor. Plus, we had had almost the same past. Now we looked into the same future together with Jesus Christ. Once a week we met to pray together. We went to meetings together. We told stories about what God was doing in our lives. Simply put – we strengthened one another!

The most important truths that should always accompany us, because they can change everything: the first one: God never changes. The Scriptures often remind us of this:

- Psalm 102:28a, *'but you are the same.'*
- Malachi 3:6, *'For I, the Lord, do not change.'*
- Hebrews 1:12b, *'But you are the same, and your years will have no end.'*
- and 13:8, *'Jesus Christ is the same yesterday, today, and forever.'*
- James 1:17, *'all good giving and every perfect gift[a] is from above, coming down from the Father of lights, with whom there is no alteration or shadow caused by change.'*

What is the significance of this for us? Enormous! Since Jesus Christ is the same today as he was two thousand years ago, I can expect him to act today just as he acted centuries ago. At one time Jesus healed the sick. What about today? If Jesus is 'the same' today, then where are the miracles and healings? I believe the key to solving this conundrum will be found in embracing the truth of God's immutability.

In my twenty-four year journey of faith, I have met many people with a half-truth. What is this truth? Let me try to explain. I call it the leper syndrome.

Once a man covered with leprosy stood before Jesus. He fell on his knees and asked Jesus with these words: *'If you wish, you can make me clean.'*[4] The literal translation reads as follows: *'If you would be willing. . .'* Herein lies the whole problem. The leper believed that Jesus could cleanse him,

---
[4]Mark 1:40–41

Chapter 7 Real signs

he knew part of the truth, but he didn't know if Jesus *wanted* to cleanse him. This is what he was missing. Jesus completes the leper's half-truth by his emphatic '***I do will it!***' The whole truth is '*I can and I will!*' That with God does not change! Many people believe that God can heal them, but how many believe the second part of that truth – that He *wants* to do it!

I have met many people over the years. I have prayed with many. Some received grace, others continued in their bondage. I don't fully know why this is happening. But I find it hard to believe that the problem lies with God. I think that it is man who somehow gets confused in his search to change his life. Józek, Romek, Krzysiek, Grzegorz, Marcin and me were not only freed from addictions. We received something even more valuable, the most precious thing that only a loving God can give. We got a new life. We were born again!

Another truth is the necessity of being born again. Jesus in John 3:3 said to a ruler of the Jews, a Pharisee: '*Amen, amen, I say to you, no one can see the kingdom of God without being born from above.*' It is true that in baptism we are born into new life with God. But it is also true that the new birth '*of water and of the Spirit,*' as Jesus teaches us, in a great multitude of the baptized is no different from their old life. Something is wrong here. Somehow this truth has escaped from us: the sacramental act of baptism has been reduced to a ceremony.

Almost all of the New Testament authors wrote about the need for the new birth, so this is very important. Why do we pass by this truth so indifferently? Why is it spoken of so little? I was baptized as an infant, and in this way I received God's new life, but for years I could not find a guidance on how to live this life! Just a baptized, unbelieving, alcohol-addicted criminal. In this condition, could I expect to see the kingdom of God?

The new life is new power. It enables us to overcome all our sinful tendencies and live according to the commandments. Through the new birth we *'may come to share in the divine nature'*.[5] My five friends I wrote about have consciously received the grace of the new birth. They have become new people. To use the biblical words – they *passed from death to life*. This was not an insignificant fact. It was a revolution!

It is the most revolutionary discovery in my life. I have not learned this anywhere else. The Lord Himself revealed to me how people have lied about the truth concerning alcoholics. This lie is that it is accepted as absolute truth to say that **'once an alcoholic – always an alcoholic.'** You can ask different experts, doctors, therapists, you will get the same answer, 'an alcoholic may not drink for five, ten, thirty years, may never reach for a glass again until the end of his life, but he will still die as an alcoholic, because being an alcoholic is forever.' Is this true or false? My answer will be surprising, but I'm convinced: both!

An alcoholic who struggles with addiction – even if he hasn't had a drink in a long time – is an alcoholic. Even if he never drinks again, he is an alcoholic. Why? Science, especially medicine, gives us the answer. Alcoholism is such a nasty and enslaving affliction that one needs to have enormous willpower, self-denial, self-control, often with the help of drugs, or even isolation, to minimize – not to remove – the power of this addiction. A person is capable of achieving this, but must be prepared for a constant struggle. Many addicts succeed in this. I have great respect and admiration

---

[5] 2 Peter 1:4b

Chapter 7 Real signs

for such people. They achieve something that I could not achieve myself. The truth is that these people control their addiction, but they don't get rid of it. The addiction is there and lurks within them, for the rest of their lives. An alcoholic who struggles with their own strength even if they get the addiction under control is an alcoholic. A very true, valid and – at the same time – sad scientific *interpretation*.

Let's look at it from a different perspective. Let's leave scientific research and experimentation for a moment and move to the level of faith. Let me use my own example. All my attempts and efforts, including therapies, aimed to fight my addiction have failed one hundred percent. Medicine was powerless. On July 6, 1989, drunk, for how could it be otherwise, with my addiction I came in prayer to Jesus. I asked Him to give me a new life, free from addictions. The next day I found out that I had not even the slightest desire for alcohol. Without any action on my part. Without any drug treatment. What happened to me?

The answer is one and most true. I was born again! The date mentioned above is the date of my new birth. I was given this new life at baptism, but until the age of thirty-eight I did not allow God to develop this life in me. But now, after deliberately surrendering to God, my new life from Him has kicked all addictions out of my body.

In St. Paul's Second Letter to Corinthians (5:17) we find an explanation for my freedom, *'So whoever is in Christ is a new creation: the old things have passed away; behold, new things have come.'*

Twenty-four years ago I invited Jesus Christ into my life. I was given a new life. My old life without Jesus, but with addictions, has passed and all things have become new. New, that is, as it had never been before, because if it had existed before, it could not have been new. In this new life I have not consciously taken a drop of alcohol into my mouth. How can I be an alcoholic? Puzzling, isn't it?

I was an alcoholic in the old life! That old life is gone! There is a new one! Am I an alcoholic? You may not agree with me. Your opinion of me, my dear Reader, will not change the God-revealed truth in me: **I am a new creation! I am not an alcoholic!**

Does my approach to alcoholism want to tear down the achievements of science? Not at all! But I don't accept the science demolishing my faith. Science has no proof that I *am* an alcoholic. The only scientific test that can confirm or deny this is if I decide to drink a serving of alcohol. And I won't do that because I don't want any alcohol in my mouth. In turn, let my proof that I am not an alcoholic continue to be the testimony of my new life.

Chapter 8
Return to family

> *Go home to your own people and tell them*
> *what the Lord has done for you,*
> *and how he has had mercy on you.*
>
> Mark 5:19

SOMETHING happened at the beginning of my homelessness that would later, after my conversion, help me to reconnect with my family. I came across a man on the street whom I had met shortly after my arrival in Hamburg. We lived for some time in the same house for displaced people. He and his brother lived in one apartment and I, then still with my wife, next door. We hanged out together. I couldn't deny, we emptied more than one can of beer together. After my wife decided to separate from me and our acquaintance has broken up. I had to move out, then she changed her address, wanting to be completely free of me.

I was homeless, had no contact with my family, didn't even know where they lived. The other day I ran into him on the street. We exchanged a few words and I found out that my wife lived in the neighborhood called *Horn*. I didn't know the exact address, but I already had a starting point. I began my search. I had a very clever plan: I would walk up the streets, from house to house, and check the names on the intercoms. It was very tedious 'work'.

Whenever I was only able to walk, I would roam around the neighborhood where my wife lived and look for her family. Not only during the day, but also at night, helping myself with a lighter, when it was too dark. All this took about three to four months. Sometimes I realized I was searching again in places I had already checked before, but I did not give up. My determination was rewarded, because finally, on one of the intercoms, I saw the name 'Krzosek'. I found the apartment where my wife lived. I made it!

I already had my family's address, but I couldn't do anything with it anyway! I was ashamed of my appearance in front of strangers, let alone my beloved ones. I was ashamed of myself in front of myself. So how could I show myself to my family in such a state? I waited a long time for my first contact with my family – until God transformed my life. And when that happened, I was eager to show myself to my wife and sons as a completely new person. I wanted to explain everything to them. To apologize. I hoped that Jola, seeing my transformation, which was real this time, would give me a chance to come back. I knew the address but I was terribly afraid to meet her. It would be easier to call, but the phone number I'd once gotten had evaporated from my memory, and the one I had saved disappeared with all my stolen documents. I had no other way. If I wanted to see my relatives, I simply had to go to them.

I was already a very happy man. I didn't drink. I had an apartment. I had a job. All I needed was a family. I believed that God would quickly take care of that too. I wanted to return to my family so much that one day, caring about nothing else, I plucked up the courage and pressed the

Chapter 8 Return to family

intercom button. Jola was at home. I said that I really had to talk to her. I had very important things to say. She answered that she wouldn't let me into her house, but if I wanted to meet her so much, she would come for a while to a cafe in a nearby shopping center. Since I was making money, I wasn't afraid of how I would pay the bill. I was prepared. I would be able to impress my wife. I was neatly dressed. I had money. I wanted her to see that I wasn't the same Henryk anymore.

We sat down at a cafe table and I began the story of my change. I said that I would like to go back to them. What Jola said was a shock to me. She had a husband and she had no intention of leaving him for me. I was supposed to forget about her. I asked, what about our children? She said I was not allowed to see them. I was not allowed to even try to enter their lives. I started insisting, explaining, clarifying. She was adamant. 'Only the court can change my decision', she said. She also added that she didn't believe I wouldn't go back to drinking. She had gotten to know me so well over the years and was well aware of the value of my promises, so it would be better if I didn't even try to convince her that things had changed in my life. And my bringing God into this was just another ploy. We drank our coffee and parted ways.

In this time I also sent a letter to my mother, who lived in Poland, 'I am here! I am alive and thank God, I am getting better!' I contacted my sisters in the same way. After some time I got an answer. My mother was happy about my conversion, however, she was concerned that it was the Roman Catholic Church. As it turned out, Jehovah's Witnesses had taken 'good care' of my mother. She joined the denomination and even decided to be re-baptized. When I wrote her that I had become a conscientious Catholic, she suggested that I should give it up and join Jehovah's Witnesses like she had, because only they were, as she put it, 'the true church'. Time has verified which of us was right.

The other day my sister Ela called me from Poland. She said she was coming to Hamburg. She would stay with Jola (I didn't even know they had been in touch), and if I wanted she could take the children and meet me. Jola had already agreed to this. And so I was able to get in touch with my sons. We started to meet.

The first meeting was even very nice, mostly thanks to my sister who tried to keep an eye on everything. The next meeting showed the enormous gap that had formed between us after years of my absence from their lives. Arek was already eleven, and Remek was six. We hadn't had any contact with each other for almost four years. I knew nothing about them. How did they develop? What friends did they have? What interested them? Little did I know. I didn't know what they knew about me. I showed up in their lives years later, and what? 'What to talk to them about? What to offer them? How will I win their hearts?' I began to realize the havoc that the separation causes in relationships with the children. 'This is something that I will never be able to fix.'

My children had a right to have me always with them. I robbed them of that privilege. I had demanded to meet my children because they were mine. But did they really want it? Or, were they only meeting with me because they had to? I will never forget the words I heard from Remek's mouth, 'Now you want to talk to me? Where were you when I wanted to talk to you?'

Every time I drove to pick up the kids I asked myself, 'Will they be happy?' I had always prayed about it before we met. And how was it? Sometimes better, sometimes worse. I think

Chapter 8 Return to family

the children sensed my fears and somehow took advantage of them by forcing me to buy them everything they wanted. I don't know, perhaps it was their right to push on dad to satisfy their whims.

Once during our meeting it was really bad. As soon as we met, Arek asked me to buy him a skateboard. They had just become fashionable. The one he chose cost about 150 marks. I didn't have that amount. We went for a walk. I suggested some activities. Remek was quick to get into it, but Arek was still sullen, he wanted the skateboard and didn't let me forget it. He manipulated me, 'I will be angry – Dad will give up.' The problem was that I had no chance to give up, because I really didn't have that much money. When I had exhausted all possibilities of pleasing Arek, I decided to drive them home. We got on the bus. Arek sat opposite to me. When I watched his gloomy face, I recalled Jesus' words about the Holy Spirit, the Comforter. I began to silently pray, 'Holy Spirit come to my son Arek and cheer him up.' Suddenly I remembered that there is an amusement park not far from the bus stop we are approaching. 'I will try just one more time. Maybe Arek will like the merry-go-round, maybe by a go-cart? We got off quickly.

Even in this place, among so many attractions, Arek was unmoved. I decided to continue the journey home. When we were leaving the amusement park, we passed by the pavilion with lottery tickets. Then the thought came to me, 'Buy them a ticket. One ticket cost three marks. It's not a fortune! Remek didn't win anything. When Arek unfolded his ticket, it read: 'FREE CHOICE.' It meant that he could choose any of the items in the lottery. I don't have to add that among the various forfeits there was also a skateboard that Arek wanted. In a moment Arek was happily walking home with his skateboard under his arm. I, on the other hand, was convinced that it's good to pray at any time, and the Holy Spirit really is the Comforter.

God has His methods of parenting and only He knows how and when to use them. In my case, God taught me through meetings with my kids. Arek made me work through the lesson about the Holy Spirit being the Comforter. Since the skateboard situation, I have never doubted it again. Whenever I was getting sad and couldn't handle it, I would be reminded of the skateboard and who it was that made both Arek and me happy. This truth still helps me overcome my sorrows.

I learned another interesting lesson from the kids. I was still a 'beginner' Christian, but even then I could see the difference between faith and logical thinking. I couldn't deal with what Jesus taught about faith, on the one hand, and what my reason told me, on the other. I wanted very much to be a believer. But, what is true faith?

The other day I met with my boys again. Arek asked me to get myself a fishing license. His friend had one and Arek wanted to join him. I agreed, but because I didn't want Remek to feel left out, I suggested that next week we would all go fishing together. I had no plan, though. I had never been fishing. I didn't think what I was talking about.

A week later, I came to pick up the kids and found out that they were already prepared for fishing. Arek bought a fishing line and a hook from his friend, Remek carved a suitable stick which was to serve as a fishing rod. And I... had forgotten all about my promise! Hiding my being surprised, I gave them the opportunity to choose the place where we would fish. This way I avoided the disaster. We went to the water and as soon as Remek put the rod down, he pulled out a small fish that he was scared of. We had a lot of fun!

Chapter 8 Return to family

Returning home, I analyzed the whole situation. My sons believed in what I had promised them a week ago. Suddenly, there came a great enlightenment in my mind, 'This is what faith is all about! They believed that I would follow my promise. They had prepared for it. They did not allow the possibility that it could be otherwise. Do I have the same faith in God? The Scriptures are full of God's promises. Do I believe what God has foretold?' I was close to have let my sons down because of my 'unbelief'. It is different with the Lord of heaven and earth. God never forgets His promises and never fails.

It wasn't until years later that I learned God's definition of faith from St Paul's Letter, *'Faith is the realization of what is hoped for and evidence of things not seen.'*[1]

My children had the certainty that we would go fishing, and we did. That certainty was my promise. They were not disappointed. We can never be disappointed in God! Although sometimes His promises conflict with our logical reasoning.

So, I eventually reconnected with my wife and children. We visited each other. As the years passed, I realized more and more that I could not infringe on their freedom. I could come to them, talk to them, have a cup of tea, but nothing more. The children had already grown up, each of them had their own life. We are separated by a great distance, not only in kilometers but also in our views on life. Jola has her own philosophy. The adult children have their own philosophy. I can't understand them and they can't understand me. I trust God and I believe that He is the only one who can make us feel like one family despite our differences.

---

[1] Hebrews 11:1

Parents and forgiveness

Looking back on my childhood and adolescence, and even the beginning of my adult life, one can conclude that my great resentment toward my parents was justified. I blamed them for my subsequent failures. Even as a believer, I faced a huge challenge with this. God required that my attitude toward my parents change, and I needed to do something about it. I wanted to follow God's commandments, but with the fourth one, that is *'Honor your father and your mother'*,[2] I had a problem. How could I honor and respect a father who had done me so much harm and caused me so much shame? How could I honor a mother who had no time for me when I needed her?

My father died in 1982. I believed that God's commandment no longer applied to me in relation to him. Whom should I honor? My father had been dead for years, and every time I remembered him, all the events that had caused the inner pain in me where coming to life. I kept asking myself, 'How could he do this to me? Why did he let this happen?'

I had no one to honor, but I still had someone to blame. Resentment, anger, and grief still accompanied me. Something didn't feel right to me here. I began to think about what would have happened if I had had a wonderful, even perfect father. How would I have behaved after his death? Would I have accepted that everything was over? Would he have become indifferent to me? Or would I still hold him in reverence and respect in my memories? I came to the conclusion that gratitude would not cease with the death of a good father, just as my pain and grief had never ceased. After making this discovery, I had to humbly accept that I

---

[2]Deuteronomy 5:16

Chapter 8 Return to family

was still bound by the fourth commandment toward my late father.

As I prayed about this and studied the Bible, my view of my father as an oppressor began to change. I could see more and more of his positive qualities in my mind. The cruel image was losing its clarity and a different image began to emerge, one that I had never seen before of a father suffering in his powerlessness. The image of a victim, not a torturer.

I used to say when I was young, 'When I have children, I will never be for them what my father was for me.' Time passed. I became a father of two boys. And as time went on, I became to my children just what my father was to me. Did I want it to be that way? No! But I was still reproducing the pattern I knew from my childhood. My father had hurt me because he himself had been hurt. Now, in turn, I was being hurt by my father – so I was hurting my children. Today I know that pain and harm can pass from generation to generation until someone breaks it.

Jesus was once asked the question, *'who sinned, this man or his parents?'*[3] I saw my parents guilty of my failures. And my father was the best fit as the culprit. And what happened in my life? I became a father and it was my turn. I inflicted the pain myself. People tend to look for someone else to blame but not themselves. My attitude was not different: everyone is to blame but me. However, the Bible tells us that *'all have sinned'*.[4] 'All' means including me!

When I realized this, I reacted immediately. As soon as it was possible I went to Szczecin, to the grave of my father. When I got there, I sat on a bench by the grave and told him everything. All my pain. All my anger. I recounted all the

---
[3] John 9:2
[4] Romans 3:23

situations I could recall. Once I got over it, I said, 'Daddy, I forgive you for all this. I realized that you wanted to be a better father for me, but you wasn't able to. You wanted to give me more love, but you couldn't because you yourself had not been given enough love. I know now that you wasn't able to give me what what you didn't have.' Then I asked to be forgiven for everything I had hurt my father with. Most of all, I asked that he forgive me for wanting him to die. I sat at the grave for a long time. Tears streamed from my eyes, I allowed myself to be healed. And I was gaining respect for my father.

I believe that there, at the cemetery, God allowed two pain-filled people to meet and gave forgiveness and reconciliation. In some strange way, my wounds that my father inflicted on me no longer hurt, no longer bleed. *'Honor your father'* is still relevant in my life today.

The situation with my mother was a little different. I remember that she always took care of me. I think she was a very fair person. She never punished me if I didn't deserve it. However, my attitude towards my mother was very negative, even though I admired her for her daily toil. I can't explain where it came from, but it was there. Maybe the resentment towards my father was the reason why my mother also got it. After all, she had chosen such a man to be my father.

I remember well my first arrival in Poland. Mom welcomed the prodigal son returning after five years with open arms. As soon as she saw me at the door of the apartment, she threw herself around my neck, hugged and kissed me. It seemed to me that this hugging will never end. I wanted to free myself from this embrace, but I couldn't. Surely Mom had put all her emotions into that hug, all the joy of getting

Chapter 8 Return to family

her son back, but I was cold as ice and wished that the affectionate welcome would end quickly.

This scene recurred every time I came home. I hated it! I didn't want her to hug me, and she kept doing it! I felt some kind of discomfort. Adding fuel to the fire was the fact that Mom, as a person of faith, was on the opposite side. As I wrote above, she had joined a Jehovah's Witness community. This I could not accept. When I visited her, I tried to be kind and helpful without letting on that I was fighting a terrible internal battle. On the one hand, I resented my mother for my unsuccessful life, but on the other, I longed for her to find the true God she had always sought, and to finally feel fulfilled and happy.

I tried many times to persuade my mother to return to the Catholic Church, but to no avail. I realized that persuading would not help, so I stopped doing it. This does not mean that I gave up; on the contrary, I simply adopted a different tactic. I no longer argued about who was right. I only talked about what God was doing in my life, in the life of the community I belonged to, in the life of the Church I attended. After a while, I began to notice that what I was saying about God was somehow working in my mother. She started asking questions. We looked into the Bible together. She went from being a know-it-all about God and the Bible – characteristic of Jehovah's Witnesses – to a truth seeker. Without even knowing, we spent together almost nine long years on our journey to reconciliation, truth, and the Church. It all ended in very tragic circumstances.

Mom went through medical examinations and was diagnosed with pancreatic cancer. The progression was really quick. Before she went to hospital, we had one more conversation. I was aware of the gravity of the situation. At any moment, a strike of the disease could prove fatal. 'Where will Mom spend eternity? Eternal life is prepared for those who will accept Jesus Christ as their Lord and Savior!' I had to act. Once again, I described to Mom what Jesus did for each person. I also said that if she accepted Jesus as God-Savior, He could heal her just as He had healed me years before. Then Mom replied, 'Son, if that were possible.' I will never forget that short sentence! Why? Because ever since that conversation I have prayed with all my strength that God would remove all her doubts and make *possible* what she thought was *not possible*. Within days, Mom was taken to hospital. Jehovah's Witnesses began visiting her in the ward.

A few years earlier, Mom had told us her will about her funeral – we were to donate her body to Jehovah's Witnesses. This was a very difficult situation for us. We didn't want to agree to this kind of burial, but we couldn't violate her will either. Our only hope was in God. We strengthened our prayer. We asked God to make Mom to see the Savior in His Son Jesus Christ.

After a short time spent in the hospital, Mom decided to cut off contact with Jehovah's Witnesses, which I learned from my sister. She refused to be visited by them, which she communicated to the leaders of the organization.

The day I had been waiting for for years finally arrived. Mom was discharged from the hospital. Not because she felt better, but on the contrary, because she felt worse and worse and medicine could no longer help. My sister Ela called me in Hamburg and said that I should come. I had already used up my vacation and there was no question of a longer stay, but I decided to come for a weekend. I took a long-distance bus to Szczecin.

Chapter 8 Return to family

During the journey I asked God for the healing of my Mother, for her conversion and that she return to the Catholic Church. I realized that in a moment I would be seeing my terminally ill Mother. What would the greeting look like? Would I be wanting to avoid hugging her, as it was before? No, I couldn't allow that anymore. I began to pray the prayer of forgiveness. It was dark and my neighbor in the seat next to me couldn't see anything, so I cried and forgave my Mom for all the hard moments in my life. When I got off the bus I was filled with love and compassion for my Mom. I longed to meet her and hug her. However, I had to wait until morning because I arrived at night and my sister persuaded me not to disturb and let Mom sleep.

The next morning I went to see her. Mom was lying in bed. She was unable to get up. She looked very weak and certainly felt that way. She had not been able to eat for some time, took only medicine. Until then, I had never felt like this in my Mother's presence. I was filled with some kind of loving compassion, but somewhere deeper – hope. I walked over to her, hugged her and kissed her on the cheek. If it had ever happened before that I kissed my mother – but I don't remember such a situation – this kiss was the first sincere one in my life. I put everything in that kiss: forgiveness, love, unity, but also my pain. Mom responded with a joyful smile. Did she feel what I wanted to convey to her? I think she did.

Around noon, Mom decided to somehow get out of bed and sat with us in her room. Then I very gently referred once again to the sacrifice of Jesus Christ, His resurrection, and our life with Him in eternity. Mom just listened. She didn't say a single word. I took courage and proposed that she accept Jesus into her life as Lord and Savior. Mom agreed. Together: Mom, sister and I prayed that the good Jesus would come to our Mother. We prayed that Jesus would heal her.

Mom wanted to speak to a priest, and her wish came true. The next day was Sunday, and I had to leave to show up for work on Monday. When I was back home after the shift on that day, my sister shared good news with me on the phone – Mom had called her into her room in the morning and said, 'Ela, Jesus has really healed me.'

What did this healing consist of? Did the disease suddenly vanish? No. Mom was still sick, but all kinds of pain associated with the illness had gone. She stopped taking medication. She began getting out of bed. Once a week, a doctor came to check on Mom and write a new prescription. When he saw Mom on her feet and she declared to him that she no longer needed any prescription, the doctor was stunned. He couldn't believe what Mom was saying. On his way out he told my sister what he thought about all this. He said that if it was true that my mother hadn't taken the medicine and yet felt so well, he had to admit it was a miracle. He would come to examine Mom several more times and on each occasion he exclaimed, 'It's a miracle!'

Mom was getting weaker and weaker though. But the weaker was her body, the stronger was her spirit, and more and more joy radiated from her face. I didn't see this because I was in Hamburg, but I heard from my sister on the phone that Mom, if she wasn't busy talking to Jesus, was telling my sister funny stories. No sadness and no anger about being sick. Five weeks after accepting Jesus into her life, our beloved Mom passed away. Before she died, she had changed her decision about the burial. She now wanted a Catholic funeral, with a Catholic priest, and to rest in the grave next to her husband, and our father.

Chapter 8 Return to family

Today I don't remember from where, but word reached us that Jehovah's Witnesses would claim Mom's body. We even feared that they might disrupt the ceremony, since several people from their organization showed up at the funeral. When the casket was taken to the cemetery chapel, we had to decide whether to keep the casket closed during the final farewell or to show Mom's body to everyone gathered. The immediate family was allowed to say goodbye in private with the coffin open. I wanted to look at Mom one last time. I had seen her face five weeks earlier when I came to visit her. Back then, her face was loaded with pain and suffering. One look at her and it was clear that her face had suffered a lot in life. This time, however, Mom's face was completely different. Her face looked as if she had always been cheerful and smiling. Such great joy emanated from that face that I had no doubt that such a face should be seen by all gathered. I also asked the priest to let me say a few words of farewell over the grave. In a few sentences I described my mother's life. She had always been looking for God, and in this search she sometimes went astray, but at the end of her life, during this lethal illness, she let God find her. She was reconciled with God and with His Son Jesus Christ. And the joy that emanates from her face is proof that in the Son of God she found the fullness of happiness. I believe she left us with joy to return to the Father's home.

So many times I have talked to my mother about God. So many times I suggested that she leave the organization she had joined. Each time to no avail. Why did she change her mind at the end of her life? I believe she needed my forgiveness and my kiss to do it.

Why forgive?

> *If you forgive others their transgressions, your heavenly Father will forgive you. But if you do not forgive others, neither will your Father forgive your transgressions.*

Matthew 6:14–15

As I described above, God has been working very intensely with me on the subject of forgiveness, and it doesn't just apply to my parents. In the Book of Ezekiel, where God talks about changing hearts, He also talks about the Holy Spirit, whose outpouring I experienced so powerfully in Switzerland during a congress. He also speaks of the ability to keep His commandments.

> *I will put my spirit within you so that you walk in my statutes, observe my ordinances, and keep them.* (Ezekiel 36:27)

I wanted very much to follow the commandments for the rest of my life. The fourth commandment, 'Honor your father and your mother,' forced me to review my previous approach to forgiveness. Once I got over it, I found that my forgiveness should have a greater reach.

When you throw a stone into water, larger and larger circles appear on the surface. Since I forgave my father, I began to understand that the range of forgiveness I should give to different people is much larger. Every now and then I would recall situations from my past in which I had been hurt. For example, the math teacher who had publicly stated that nothing good would come of me. Suddenly, so many years later, I recall his name – the only teacher's name I

Chapter 8 Return to family

remembered. I knew that God wanted something from me, and that something was to forgive those who had hurt me in various ways. Did I want to forgive? Certainly not. That's because I didn't want to revisit the wrongs I had suffered, because the memories kept triggering bad emotions and shame in me.

When I was gathering the list of people who have wronged me, I suddenly made an amazing discovery, 'I am on someone's list too! How many people have something against me? How many people have I hurt? How many people have I used for my purposes? How many have I let down in their expectations? How many have I cheated? How many have I robbed? I am on the same scales as my abusers and tormentors!' If God were to apply His righteous law, I would be standing in the dock with all those who abused me, robbed me, let me down, or hurt me in any other way.

We are all equal. *'There is no one just, not one'*, St. Paul wrote to the Romans (3:10b), and added further, *'all have sinned'* (3:23a). And Jesus says, *'if you do not forgive others, neither will your Father forgive your transgressions'*.[5] I didn't have to think any longer. It occurred to me that forgiveness begets forgiveness, and I wanted to be forgiven. Most of all, I wanted to remain in the forgiveness that comes from and through God.

I decided to forgive everyone and forever, but the question remained, how I should do it. I was not able to reach all the people I should have forgiven. What to do in this situation? What action, if any, should I take? I made up my mind to forgive and that's all right, but is that all I can do? Once again, Jesus Himself came in His word and helped me by reminding what is written in the Gospel of Matthew:

---

[5] Matthew 6:15

Henryk Krzosek ❧ GOD FOUND ME ON THE STREET

But I say to you, love your enemies, and pray for those who persecute you (5:44)

I still didn't know how to love my enemies at that time. But I could try to pray. I chose my greatest enemy. The number one enemy in my life. I didn't feel like praying for him, but if I was supposed to pray, let it be the top enemy. I felt that this is what God expected of me. It wasn't easy.

When I was only a teenager, my friends and I used to go to the woods. During summer vacations, the forest was full of attractions. We climbed trees. We jumped into a mid-forest lake – usually in places where it was forbidden to swim. We lounged in the sun on the bank of the lake, competing for the best tan on our backs. The other day an adult man joined us and lay down on his blanket next to us. Somehow he quickly struck up a conversation with us and started inventing various interesting games. The sun was setting and we had to go home. Then the man suggested that we meet here the next day, and certainly he will prepare something attractive for us. Of course, we readily agreed.

The next day he told us a lot about himself. I was fascinated by the fact that he was a driver of a big truck. At one point he asked if I would like to drive the truck with him. I had never ridden in a truck like that before, and I had never ridden next to the driver. I wanted it very much. I agreed to go with him. I waited for him near the place where I lived. Excitedly, I looked out for any truck coming, until finally my 'friend' arrived. We were delivering some goods to the stores and I was very proud to be sitting next to the driver of such a big truck. Unfortunately, that day my driver had to quickly say goodbye to me because he was in a hurry. We agreed to meet another day.

Chapter 8 Return to family

As I waited for the next meeting, I thought about my father, 'Why is he not as good to me as this man I recently met?' If possible, I would swap my father for this man, who cared about me. What I didn't realize at the time was that this guy was thinking about me too. He had his own secret plans. Soon after he gained my trust, he moved on and sexually abused me in a cruel way. I didn't know how to act. I could not defend myself. I was terribly afraid, but I was helpless. My only desire was to get away from this man as fast and as far as possible. I managed to escape, but the trauma remained. For a long time I was afraid that I might meet him somewhere on the street. For fear of that encounter, I avoided the street from where he would take me to his truck. As I grew up, the fear of meeting him turned into a desire for revenge.

A few years later I met him on the street. I was an adult now. I believed that this was the time for my revenge. I just didn't know how to get it. I started following him. I wanted to see where he would go. A few blocks away he entered one of the buildings. I ran up quickly and saw him enter a first floor apartment. I didn't know if he lived here or maybe he just came to visit someone. To check it out I waited until late at night. I found some bricks and put them under the window where the light was on. I climbed onto the windowsill and saw the man I hated in the kitchen. I plotted my revenge: I would burn down the apartment with him inside. I didn't know yet how to do it, but I decided to think it over and plan it well.

I hadn't yet had time to fully develop a plan for revenge, because I was caught in another crime. I found myself in jail. I had to postpone my revenge. After two years, I was released. The desire for revenge faded a little, but it didn't die. I thought I would have to come back to it at some point, but not yet. Now was the time to enjoy my newly regained freedom.

Taking advantage of this freedom, I went with my friends to a nearby bar. We sat down at a table and I checked the company sitting at other tables. At a table near the wall sat the man I hated. I was paralyzed by this sight, but the desire for revenge returned. I couldn't do anything, though. I pretended not to see him. Who knows, maybe he was acting that way too. Out of the corner of my eye, I noticed that the man now had scars on his face. I figured something must have happened to him. That satisfied me, but not completely. I was the one who was going to inflict the most suffering on him. I believed that this was the only way I could take away my pain and shame. After a while the man left, and I started thinking again about how to burn down his apartment.

But situation repeated itself. I was hindered from inflicting punishment by another term of imprisonment, this time a longer one – five years. After I was released and started a family, I gave up on such spectacular revenge, but I believed that there would come a time when I would come face to face with my abuser. If it came to that, I would not hesitate. Unfortunately, I went abroad and the an occasion never came.

Then there was my conversion and gave my life to Jesus, and Jesus was saying *'Forgive!'* However, in this case it was unthinkable. Good that Jesus left me a little wicket by also saying, *'Pray for your enemies'*. In this aspect, I was able to take some minimal action. I started praying that, not me, but God would bless this man. Whenever I would think back to the situation, I would say to God, 'Lord, bless this man'. Just a routine prayer. And here, one time, without any hesitation, I fired out: 'Lord, I bless this man.' When I realized what I had just said, I was stunned! I continued to pray for my

Chapter 8 Return to family

enemy. And you know what, it didn't even begin to hurt! My enemy became closer and closer to me, and the negative emotions associated with him grew weaker and weaker. It took a couple of years.

The other day I came by car to Szczecin, and I wanted to have my car repaired. I was recommended a garage located on street where my abuser used to live. I parked my car along the sidewalk and was about to get out when I saw the man walking towards me up the street. He was an old man now, and if it weren't for the scars on his face, I probably wouldn't have recognized him at all. Everything came rapidly back to me. There was only one thing missing – I didn't feel the desire for revenge! I bowed my head in prayer and happily thanked God that He had taught me to forgive. When I lifted my head a moment later, that man was gone.

I don't know if my forgiveness and my prayers transformed this man. But I do know that praying for him transformed me. This last encounter made me realize that through forgiveness I have become a free man. I got rid of a great burden that I had been carrying for so many years. It was as if a big and heavy backpack was taken off me, which contained pain, fear, hatred, powerlessness, desire for revenge, shame. I had been walking with that backpack for almost fifty years of my life. I never parted with it during the day, I went to bed with it at night. Has anyone tried sleeping with a backpack? That is how I felt, it was due to lack of forgiveness. In such a state I would certainly die if not for Christ and His commandment: *'love your enemies, and pray for those who persecute you'*.

I have also learned two great truths about the need to forgive. One is that I hurt myself by not forgiving. And the other truth is contained in the fact that I, too, need forgiveness. We are all equal. If someone had the right to say that some injuries cannot be forgiven, it would be me. But God has taught me one more thing: with Him, we can forgive anyone! Even more! Not only to forgive, but also to fulfill Jesus' expectations: *'Love your enemies'*. Of course, we can't do that on our own. We have no business even trying.

Saint Paul in his Letter to the Romans (5:5) paved the way for us to love our enemies by revealing to us that *'hope does not disappoint, because the love of God has been poured out into our hearts through the holy Spirit that has been given to us.* It is not our limited and volatile affection that we can love our enemies with, but God's love that He pours into our hearts. A new heart and God's love in it – that is the effective way to forgiveness.

Chapter 9

Bible – the instruction manual to life

> *My son, to my words be attentive,*
> *to my sayings incline your ear;*
> *Let them not slip from your sight,*
> *keep them within your heart;*
> *For they are life to those who find them,*
> *bringing health to one's whole being.*
>
> Proverbs 4:20–22

WHERE did my fascination with the Bible begin and where did it come from? There is no one comprehensive answer to this question. I think it was a process that began in my childhood. From the perspective of my life today, I would venture to say that God had been preparing me for years for the work in which He wanted me to participate.

In the fourth grade of elementary school I was given my first Holy Scripture by a classmate and yard friend. Granted, it was only the Gospel of John and was probably the translation adopted by Jehovah's Witnesses, but it was the first biblical text I came across. I remember my sister Ela and I reading the passage together:

Henryk Krzosek ⌇ GOD FOUND ME ON THE STREET

In the beginning was the Word,
and the Word was with God,
and the Word was God.[1]

We burst out laughing without understanding anything of it. And even though this Gospel made us laugh and we had no idea that it was the Word of God, I still remember the little book that a friend gave me.

Many years passed and I still had no personal relation with the Bible. When I found myself in Germany, one of my buddies told me how he was deceiving a German preacher, who wanted to convert him with the Bible. He was using the preacher's gullibility and kept getting some money out of him. I don't know why, but I asked him to get the Scriptures for me from this pastor. I wanted to know them.

While in prison, I started reading books. Later, the Bible was also on my reading list. I was very curious about what I would find in it. I started from the first page and read voraciously until I reached the book of Numbers. But I was getting more and more bored with what I was reading. I had no idea what it was all about. I decided there was no point in going on. I suggested to the buddy that he give back the Preacher his Bible because I wasn't finding anything interesting in it.

The time came when I ended up in a German jail. To kill the boredom, I visited the prison library. I wanted to find something to read there. The only book in Polish that I found there was the Bible. I took it and went back to my cell. I started again with the first book and the first chapter. I think I read more out of boredom than out of curiosity, although I must say that some stories caught my attention. I especially enjoyed the characters of the great men such as Moses,

---
[1] John 1:1

Chapter 9 Bible – the instruction manual to life

Samson, David, and the Maccabees brothers. Learning about their stories I thought, 'I wish I could be like that too'.

I got to the book of Job. As I was reading his story, I realized that God chooses some and supports them, but since He contributed to Job's misery, He must be a very cruel God. I wanted nothing to do with Him. What guarantee did I have that He would not deal with me the way He did with Job?

Three attempts to read the Bible failed. You could say that each time I told God: 'No!' However, that fourth, breakthrough moment came. At the restaurant for the homeless, I was given this tiny New Testament. In it, I began to see God in a different light. No longer as a bloody, war-mongering cruelty, but as a loving Father who gave His Son for me. What else did I find there? I learned that He wants to make my life fruitful. I declared, 'God, if you can and will, take my alcohol-soaked life and use it for your glory.' God took my statement seriously. He took possession of me, and His Word became the content of my life.

As I read through the Bible twice, cover to cover, I began to realize why I had failed so much in my life, why nothing was working out the way I had planned. Simply put, I was living a broken life, and I couldn't fix it in any way. Where did the mistake lie?

For a long time I was going to work by bike. Finally, my old bicycle refused to work. The hub in the rear wheel began to jam. I decided to play mechanic. After all, I am a locksmith. I disassembled and reassembled many more complicated machines in my life than a bicycle wheel. I brought the wheel home and set about fixing it. While disassembling, the balls came out of the bearing. I took the hub apart and, not finding the cause of the failure, tried to reassemble it. Here a complication arose. I could not place the balls in their previous location. After several attempts, I gave up. In this way the wheel stayed in the room for a month. Finally, having no idea how to put it back together, I took the wheel with all the disassembled parts and went to a bicycle repair shop. When the bike repairman looked at what I had brought, he said that it could not be repaired. You have to replace the whole wheel with a new one. What did I learn from my experience with the broken wheel? First of all, that if something is broken, you have to go to a professional. In the case of the bicycle, it was a mechanic. But where do you go with your broken life?

Until the age of thirty-eight I always acted as I did with the bicycle wheel – I wanted to fix my life by myself. We know what the result was. When life breaks down, we cannot fix it ourselves! That is the truth! What do we do then? When our abilities fail, we ask other people for help. But do we think about the fact that the lives of the people we seek help from usually do not function normally either? For example, a couple in crisis goes to a psychologist and asks for help. It turns out that this consultant, who is supposed to help, is in the process of a second divorce. He was unable to help himself, and he is supposed to help others. Jesus very emphatically said, *'If a blind person leads a blind person, both will fall into a pit'*[2]. I have nothing against psychologists, they are very needed, but if I were to see one, I would seek one whose life is grounded in God.

Why is it that when a piece of equipment that is under warranty breaks down, we send it back to the manufacturer? Because only the maker is the competent institution to repair it effectively. Because they know how the product was

---

[2]Matthew 15:14

Chapter 9 Bible – the instruction manual to life

designed. The giver and guarantor of our life is God. When something breaks in life, we should go to see Him. Unfortunately, some people believe that they evolved from a monkey, in which case it would be foolish to seek help from a monkey. People who do not believe in the fatherhood of God will never find their Life-Giver. Who are they supposed to go to if crisis comes? They are on their own, and their lives get jammed up like the broken hub of my bicycle wheel.

What did the Life-Giver do when I came to him? First of all, He said that my life is not repairable. The only solution is a new life, which God does not deny to anyone who comes to Him. And so I became owner of a new life, a life without any defects or faults. But beware, this new life is without flaws or faults only at the moment we receive it! Over time it wears out, just like everything else. In order to prolong the life of a device, the manufacturer includes an instruction manual. By following the instructions, we can enjoy a long life of the item. If we do not look into the manual, we may run into trouble.

Let me use an example. We have installed a dishwasher in the kitchen of our New Evangelization Center in Witkowo Drugie, near Szczecin. As the Center is visited by many people, many of them use the dishwasher. One time we ran out of dishwasher tablets. There were a lot of dirty dishes, so someone placed them in the dishwasher and, not finding any tablets, poured some regular washing-up detergent. When the dishwasher was turned on, it almost exploded. Foam was coming out by all possible means. The end result was that we had to buy a new dishwasher. Why did the user make such a big mistake? There is only one answer – they had not read the relevant instruction manual.

And how does this relate to life? Does life have an instruction manual? If so, where can it be found? God has 'manufactured' our lives, and He has attached an instruction manual to His 'product'. This, of course, is the Bible! When I began to follow it, everything began to change in me and around me. Life became more meaningful. I finally began to understand who I was and where I should go. The most beautiful adventure of my life began.

God, M.D.

In the 'Koinonia John the Baptist' community, there is a strong emphasis on one hour of personal prayer and reading at least one chapter of the Bible each day. Through this I have discovered the healing power of God's Word and personal prayer. Reading Psalm 1 I learned about the need to meditate on God's Word not only during the day, but also at night. If we do so, God provides us with a fruitful life. I thought I had to do something about it, and I did. Once a week I devoted an hour at night to pray and meditate on the Word. Although it was difficult for me to get up in the middle of the night to pray, the effort made prayer more and more enjoyable.

One night, when the scheduled hour had passed and I still wanted to pray, I thought about whether to try an all-night prayer vigil. After all, I still lived near a church to which I had keys. I could ask the pastor for permission to pray in the church at night at any time. Of course he agreed. I chose a specific time, from Friday 10 pm. to Saturday five am.

When I opened the side door of the church at night and went inside, I realized that I had not made arrangements with the pastor to keep the lights on. Then I was still terrified of the dark. This fear had accompanied me through life since childhood. As an adult, I always made sure that there was

Chapter 9 Bible – the instruction manual to life

a night lamp at my bedside. Always, when I went to sleep in the evening, first I closed my eyes and then I turned off the light. In the morning it was the other way round – first I would blindly find the switch and turn on the light, and then I would open my eyes.

Now inside the church I had a problem. What to do? Common sense told me that I should not turn on the light. I had a choice: either give up praying or stay in the dark church. Maybe because there were some candles lit in the side aisle, I chose the latter. I closed the door behind me, sat down in a pew and, without opening my eyes, began to pray. I was constantly aware of the darkness around me. Although my eyes were closed, I knew that eventually I would have to open them. And then what? I prayed with all my might that nothing would happen!

Suddenly, I heard a rustling in the pew behind me. My hair stood on end. Then there was a knock – I thought it was in the choir loft. It was followed by another noise, and some other sounds. 'What is going on! Am I not alone in this church? Are these ghosts?'

My salvation was the candles still lit. I went to where they were standing. I sat down and began to read the Bible. In this way, by this faint light, I wanted to get away from the reality that surrounded me. I read and prayed, prayed and read. Finally, the last candle went out. I sat for a long time with my eyes closed. But I had to open them eventually. At first I gently looked only under my feet. Then I dared to raise my eyes to the altar. Slowly I began to distinguish the shapes. I saw the tabernacle. 'Here is the living Jesus. So close to me. Forget the sounds in the pews and in the choir. Jesus is here!' That's how I persevered until morning.

That night my phobia vanished. I was completely freed from that horrible fear that had enslaved me for so many years. One could say that I once was dying of fear of the dark, and by meditating on God's Word, I drew new life from it. Today I know that Word: *'My son, concentrate attentively on my words...for they are life to those who find them and provide health to their entire being'* is supremely effective and powerful.

Fear of darkness lies in the non-material sphere of man. The psychic sphere, entangled by any phobia, does not allow a person to develop life to the full. In my case it was the fear of darkness. I lived and I did not live. It was only in Jesus Christ, as the Word, that I found another life in my psyche, free from fear.

God has arranged it in such a way that man, besides his mental life, also has a physical life, that is, a body. The body is subject to all kinds of weaknesses, above all, illnesses. The final line of Proverbs quoted as the motto of this chapter (4:20–22), instructs us that God's Word is also the *medicine of our whole body*. How does this apply to my life? I learned this text by heart many years ago. When I stand for morning prayer and Bible study, I often quote this very text, asking God that as I read and meditate on the Word, His life will flow into me and heal every sick cell in my body.

When I was 59 years old, at the place where I was employed, I was washing various machines and equipment with solvent. Most likely, I was poisoned, because at one point I lost my balance for a moment. When I returned home, this situation repeated itself. The next day, full of anxiety, I went to the doctor. I was referred to a neurologist. After initial tests, I was suspected of having carotid artery stenosis. I was referred for an ultrasound of the arteries and other tests to show my overall health. After all the tests were done, I returned with the results to the neurologist who diagnosed

Chapter 9 Bible – the instruction manual to life

me. When she reviewed the documents, she asked how old I was. I said I was fifty-nine. She asked if I had already my 59th birthday. I replied that not yet. She said that she would write in my medical record (or in my case, my health record) that I was fifty-eight years old, because from the results I provided her, I shouldn't even be that old. For my age I had outstandingly good test parameters.

Today I still enjoy good health, and I believe that my health comes from believing that God's Word is effective and does exactly what it says it does. Of course, I too sometimes get sick. When that happens, I may need a treatment, but I never forget that God is my primary care physician. In the Book of Exodus (15:26), God says:

> *If you listen closely to the voice of the Lord, your God, and do what is right in his eyes: if you heed his commandments and keep all his statutes, I will not afflict you with any of the diseases with which I afflicted the Egyptians; for* **I, the Lord, am your healer.**

It is clear from this text that God wants to be my doctor. He is my Father! He wants me to be healthy! However, He can only help me if I seek help from Him. In another place God said: '*I will remove sickness from your midst*'.[3] A few books further on, in Deuteronomy (7:15), we come across the same promise: '*The Lord will remove all sickness from you*'.

God cannot act contrary to what He has promised. If it were otherwise – we could call God a liar, and that is incomprehensible and unacceptable. But, notice, our Lord and Creator did not promise that we would not get sick! He

---
[3] Exodus 23:25b

has promised to give away sickness from us. For how long? Until the next disease strikes. Here I see a great relationship between God and my health – I will constantly be attacked by disease and various ailments, so I constantly need to come to God as my primary physician.

God the Father is my GP, my primary care physician. I go to Him first when I'm sick and He either heals me or refers me to an earthly doctor for further treatment.

Let me quote a few verses from the Wisdom of Ben Sira (38:1), '*Make friends with the doctor, for he is essential to you;* **God has also established him in his profession.**' God has not usurped the exclusive right to heal illnesses. He often wants to heal through the hands of earthly doctors, acting as if in the background. In the verses (38:9–13) that follow we find confirmation of this:

> *My son, when you are ill, do not delay, but pray to God, for it is he who heals.*
>
> *Flee wickedness and purify your hands; cleanse your heart of every sin.*
>
> *Offer your sweet-smelling oblation and memorial, a generous offering according to your means.*
>
> *Then give the doctor his place lest he leave; you need him too,*
>
> **For there are times when recovery is in his hands.**

Very often I come across the statement: 'If God loved me, He would not have allowed my sickness'. When I hear something like that, I feel helpless. After all, we live in a fallen world. At the very beginning of creation, God said that He was giving us possession of the whole earth and we were to

Chapter 9 Bible – the instruction manual to life

rule over it. Unfortunately, our first parents, Adam and Eve, gave this dominion to the adversary of God and man, Satan, whom St. Paul in 2 Corinthians (4:4) calls *'the god of this world'* who blinds the minds of men.

How blind must be the minds of people who blame God for illnesses and other misfortunes. It does not take much effort to discover that such thinkers do not look into the revelation contained in the Bible. If they did, they would find the following:

> *Do not court death by your erring way of life,*
> *nor draw to yourselves destruction by the works of your hands.*
>
> *Because God did not make death,*
> *nor does he rejoice in the destruction of the living.*
>
> *For he fashioned all things that they might have being,*
> *and the creatures of the world are wholesome;*
>
> *There is not a destructive drug among them*
> *nor any domain of Hades on earth.* (Wisdom 1:12–14)
>
> *For God formed us to be imperishable;*
> *the image of his own nature he made us.*
>
> *But by the envy of the devil, death entered the world.* (Wisdom 2:23–24a)

Death, and therefore disease, is not an invention of God! It is a consequence of disobedience to God! What to do in such a situation? This is what I am writing about: accept the fact that sickness will come, and when it comes, above all seek help from God, and not turn away from Him in anger, as one of kings of Judah, Asa, did. Let me cite this passage because it is very telling.

> *In the thirty-ninth year of his reign, Asa contracted disease in his feet; it became worse, but even with this disease he did not seek the Lord, only physicians. Asa rested with his ancestors; he died in the forty-first year of his reign.* (2 Chronicles 16:12–13)

The opposite to such unwise conduct is found in the attitude of another king of Judah, Hezekiah. Hezekiah became deathly ill and in his sickness cried out to the Lord. What was God's response to Hezekiah's prayer?

> *I have heard your prayer; I have seen your tears. Now I will add fifteen years to your life.* (Isaiah 38:5)

The choice is ours. God's law established centuries ago still applies whether we want it to or not. In Deuteronomy we read:

> *See, I have today set before you life and good, death and evil. If you obey the commandments of the Lord, your God, which I am giving you today, loving the Lord, your God, and walking in his ways, and keeping his commandments, statutes and ordinances, you will live and grow numerous.* (Deuteronomy 30:15–16a)

And also further:

> *If, however, your heart turns away and you do not obey, but are led astray and bow down to other gods and serve them, I tell you today that you will certainly perish; you will not have a long life...* (Deuteronomy 30:17–18a)

Chapter 9 Bible – the instruction manual to life

The blessing is: *'you will live and grow numerous'*. Here we have to touch on a very controversial topic – fertility. We know that there is a demographic decline in Poland and other countries. Fewer and fewer children are born. Schools are being closed. The society has somehow lost its way and is looking for a rescue. Looking into the statistics I found out that infertility is a disease of the civilization of the twenty-first century. Every fifth couple in Poland cannot become parents. One of the proposed methods of dealing with infertility is the IVF procedure, which arouses so much controversy. And God said to the first people, *'Be fertile and multiply'*.[4] There is something even more revolutionary in the book of Exodus[5]:

> *I will remove sickness from your midst; no woman in your land will be barren or miscarry.*

One could exclaim, 'Wait a minute, Henryk! Are you saying that God determines fertility and infertility?' Yes, that's exactly right. God gives fertility, even when someone is medically infertile.

Be fertile – three 'cases'

I fondly recall the birth of my godson, Samuel. Iza, his Mom, faced the doctors' opinion during her pregnancy that she would not carry the pregnancy to term. Samuel, in the most optimistic scenario, will be born prematurely. In the sixth month of pregnancy Izabella was admitted to the hospital, where she worked as a midwife. All the doctors taking care

---

[4] Genesis 1:28
[5] Exodus 23:25b–26a

of her in the hospital were her colleagues. They all said that there was no way the child would be born at the right time.

One day, I visited Isa in the hospital. She reached for her Bible and showed me God's promise recorded in the book of Exodus. She said that she prays this Word over and over again and believes that she will give birth to Samuel without complications at the right time.

I returned home and started calling members of our community asking them to pray that Isa would not give birth prematurely. The whole community surrounded her with prayer. Days passed. Weeks passed. One month, then another, and Iza was still not in labor. Doctors, more and more puzzled, kept visiting her, shaking their heads.

Finally the day came, when the pregnancy should normally end with childbirth, according to all medical books. Still, Iza did not give birth on that day. It was not until a few days later when healthy Samuel was born. God heard our prayers and once again proved that He does not disappoint.

The friends whose wedding I described earlier, Bożena and Krzysiek Moćko (read the story of Krzysiek's healing on page 122), also experienced God's extraordinary intervention. But let me start from the beginning. We went our separate ways for a few years. One day Father Ireneusz sent me an invitation to celebrate the tenth anniversary of the 'Diakonia of Evangelization'. I had been there from the very beginning and I really wanted to participate in this celebration.

I arrived in Carlsberg a bit late. There was already a service in the chapel to start the celebration. I entered the chapel quietly and, standing at the very end, I began to look around curiously in search of my old friends. At some

Chapter 9 Bible – the instruction manual to life

point I saw Bożena and Krzysiek. Then, out of nowhere, this thought came across my mind: 'They are going to have a baby next year'. I already knew a little about the gifts of the Holy Spirit. One of them is 'the gift of knowledge'. I didn't associate that thought with the gift at that time, but the future showed that it was indeed. I felt something that later became a reality.

After the service and greeting our friends we sat down on the couch with Krzysiek and Bożena to share the news of what was going on with whom. Then I heard that they had been trying for a child for years and nothing came out. Their visits to gynecologists were briefly described by Bożena: 'treating everything else, they didn't treat infertility'. In this state of affairs they decided to have private payable therapy by an endocrinologist. I then told them of my thought when I saw them in chapel. Although up to that point, there were still intense prayers going on for their conception, I suggested that we pray for a child from now on, holding on to God's promise that in His people *'no woman will be barren'*.

The celebration ended and we dispersed to our homes. Later I learned that the doctor–endocrinologist, after almost a year of fruitless treatment, proposed a procedure to unclog the fallopian tubes. When they were about to decide, it turned out that Bożena was pregnant! When the doctor heard about it, he jokingly said that Bożena must have been so afraid of the surgery that something 'unlocked' in her body. One year after our conversation in Carlsberg, a girl Dominika was born. This name means 'belonging to the Lord'. Her parents became absolutely convinced that only the Lord is the giver of life and every life belongs to Him. Later, a son was born to them, Matthew, just like the first

Evangelist. With this name he was to testify that the Gospel is the truth of God.

Another story is about my other friends, Krysia and Maciek Miśkiewicz, who live in Hamburg. Today they have three wonderful children, and looking at them, you could say they are fulfilled in parenting. But those who know them, know how great a battle they had to fight for the life of their youngest child – Jakub. Their faith was tested in fire. Maciek himself put it this way: 'We were in the middle of a cyclone'. Everything started happily. They wanted to have a third child. Krysia became pregnant. But at the very beginning of the pregnancy she felt very bad. She went through examinations. The diagnosis was unequivocal and devastating. No fetal waters were found. The baby in such circumstances has no chance to survive to term. The doctors unanimously stated that the pregnancy had to be terminated within the days.

The parents notified all their friends about what was happening and asked for prayers. When the news reached me, I was shocked. After all, they were my friends! As I prayed, I kept reminding myself of the truth from the book of Wisdom, which says that *'God did not make death'* and *'he fashioned all things that they might have being'*. 'God did not create a new life in Krysia's womb just to put it to death!', I thought and prayed this way.

'You formed my inmost being; you knit me in my mother's womb.'[6] David wrote these beautiful words! Would God start to form and knit a new man only to immediately kill him? No, I did not allow such thoughts to enter my mind. I went to see Krysia and Maciek at the hospital. Maciek told me about

---
[6]Psalm 139:13

Chapter 9 Bible – the instruction manual to life

everything that had happened to them and shared with me something unbelievable. Every day the doctors convinced them that because of the lack of fetal waters, the baby had no room and could not move. But each time Maciek and Krysia put their hands on her belly to pray, they felt the baby move.

The doctors were impatient and insisted on a firm, unambiguous decision from the parents. The parents, however, decided that the pregnancy would not be terminated. Surrounded by a lot of praying people, grounded in faith, they waited for what the next days would bring. After several weeks of struggle, prayer and pain, Jacob was born. As a premature baby, he was placed in the perinatal intensive care unit. Examinations showed no other complications that should have occurred due to the lack of fetal waters. During the pregnancy, the ultrasound always showed far too little water. Under such conditions, the baby's internal organs could not develop properly. But it was enough for Jacob. *'Whoever had little did not have less'*.[7] God *formed* properly all the child's organs, his *inmost being*, whether the conditions were favorable or not. Only He is able to do that!

Today Jacob is five years old. He is a remarkably healthy child. His incredible birth is a riddle for medicine. The case was studied and published in various medical journals, always with a question mark. For his parents and for all of us who prayed for Jacob's life – everything is clear. God, the giver of life, is still in control of every life!

---

[7] 2 Corinthians 8:15

One flesh

In God's design, fertility is reserved only for married couples. Marriage is an institution invented by God, not by man. Even at the beginning of creation, when there was only Adam in the world, God was preparing him to be introduced to another person – even though the other person did not yet exist. I love Adam's first meeting with Eve. Look at his delight, *'This one, at last, is bone of my bones and flesh of my flesh;'*[8] Adam recognized his destiny. God knew this beforehand, but He had to prepare Adam for it. How did He do that?

At one point, God mysteriously states: *'It is not good for the man to be alone'*[9], but the man himself does not yet know that he *is* alone. Before God introduces Eve to Adam, He has to arouse in him a desire for another person. How does the action unfold? God brings all creatures to the man so that the man can give them names. This directly follows God's statement about Adam's being alone. Why? Apart from Adam's naming every living thing, God must have had another plan. Was seeing all creatures supposed to open Adam's eyes to his loneliness?

Once man realized how lonely he was, God moved into action – He put Adam to sleep and created a woman from his rib. When Adam opened his eyes, he saw someone who was a perfect match for him, someone he had already surely dreamed of. 'I'm not alone anymore! I have someone to share my life with!' *'That is why a man leaves his father and mother and clings to his wife, and the two of them become one body.'*[10]

---
[8] Genesis 2:23
[9] Genesis 2:18
[10] Genesis 2:24

Isn't that wonderful! Only in God's mind could such a thing be born. A woman was made from a man. Human from human. God planned for man to return to where he was taken from. They would join together and be one flesh again. That is the institution of marriage! God only separated woman from man for a 'moment' to re-establish them as one flesh through marriage. A woman and a man. In Adam, God made a separation in order to make a permanent union.

However, after original sin, man continues to try to interfere with God's authority. Unfortunately, the results are disastrous. Man separates what God has joint together. Man has usurped the right to decide how marriage should be. He has established laws and regulations that in essence provide no guarantee of the permanence of marriage. The society we live in prepares young couples for divorce, not for a lasting relationship. There are no regulations that would protect the stability of marriage. On the other hand, there are a lot of regulations facilitating effective divorce. Moses already had a big problem with this and under pressure instituted a 'letter of divorce'. Was this in accordance with God's will? Absolutely not! That's why Jesus restored God's original intention. *'So they are no longer two, but one flesh. Therefore, what God has joined together, no human being must separate.'*[11] How far mankind today has departed from the 'instruction manual to life' concerning marriage.

Life is all about decisions

It may be strange, but it was only in studying the Bible that it occurred to me that life is a string of overlapping decisions. We make right decisions and wrong decisions. Good and bad.

---

[11] Matthew 19:6

God constantly encourages us to do certain things, but He also warns us not to do others.

In my marriage, my wife required me to make decisions. My most frequent response was, 'You decide.' I lacked certainty in everything. What I didn't realize was that by running away from making decisions, I was making a decision not to decide. And it was a very bad decision!

Good decisions and bad decisions. There are no neutral ones. Every decision I make affects my life now and in the future. For example, if we bend a piece of paper in half, even after ironing it, there will be a bend left – an irreversible mark. A decision cannot be erased. A bent piece of paper has two sides. On one side this bend is convex, and on the other concave. Something convex is positive because it directs the mind toward addition. The opposite is something concave. The concave subtracts. Decisions either add something to life or take something away from life. I used to not think about that at all. And God wants people to make good decisions that add something positive to life. He wants to help us in this. He wants to tell us which decision is right. We are not alone in all this – we have the Holy Spirit: *'The Advocate, the holy Spirit that the Father will send in my name—he will teach you everything and remind you of all that I told you.'*[12]

So when does the Holy Spirit remind us of all that Jesus said? In the moment of decision making. I used to be afraid of making decisions because I felt alone in it. Now I know that the Holy Spirit is with me. But beware, the Holy Spirit **reminds** us! To 'remind' something means that we have to know this in the first place. He '*will remind you of **all that I told you**.*' We have to hear it from Jesus in the first place. In what way? First of all, by reading God's Word. '*In the*

---

[12] John 14:26

Chapter 9 Bible – the instruction manual to life

beginning was the Word, and the Word was with God, and the Word was God.' The *'Word'* here is Jesus, and when we read that Word, He speaks to us. Jesus speaks and we forget. That's okay! The most important thing is that we seek Jesus in the Word. When we are forced to make a decision, the Holy Spirit will remind us of what we once read.

And there is even more: *'But when he comes, the Spirit of truth, he will ... declare to you the things that are coming.'*[13] I no longer have to worry about my future! God has the best plan for me, that is His will. And He wants to reveal this plan to me through the Holy Spirit. I don't have to go down the deceptive and destructive road of consulting fortune-tellers and reading horoscopes. Through the Holy Spirit, God's way of knowing the future is very secure.

There was a time in my life when the thought of living someday in 'a mansion with a swimming pool' kept coming back to me. I know it didn't come from me because I didn't desire anything like that. I thought and still think that a big house would be a burden for me. But this was a time when I was still persistently praying for my family to be restored, and in such a situation a large house would be very useful, and having a pool would not be 'a bad idea'. During one of my walks with my wife I shared this thought with her. She commented, 'Since you started believing in God, you've been such a dreamer.'

It has been a year and a half since that walk. Whenever the thought of a house with a pool popped up in my head, I would quickly suppressed it. The other day my sister called. Her voice sounded serious. She said she had something important to tell me. I was scared at first because I didn't know what she meant. What was this serious conversation

---
[13] John 16:13

supposed to be about? My sister got right to the point, 'My husband and I want to buy a house.' I had no objection to that. If they could only afford such a purchase, go ahead. Then she said that they wanted to buy this house together with me. This was where the big problem came in. I had not planned to buy any house, if only for the reason that I had no money. And I wasn't thinking about returning to Poland yet. So why would I need a house?

Then my sister presented me with the plan they had already worked out with Jacek, her husband. They had the opportunity to buy a large house for relatively little money. The house had four stories plus a basement with a garage. The sister's plan was as follows: I would have the first floor, where there is a one-bedroom apartment with a kitchen and a bathroom, and my sister and her husband and son would settle on the upper floors. There are two separate entrances, so we won't disturb each other. To carry out this plan, they will take a loan and I will contribute to its repayment to the best of my ability. Another argument in my sister's hand was the fact that I had always stayed with them when I visited Szczecin. Their apartment was very small and every time I came, their son Marek would have to move to his parents' bedroom to sleep on a mattress, because I occupied his bedroom. Buying a house was supposed to solve this problem.

These arguments did not convince me. I had no intention of going into it. However, my enthusiastic sister decided to describe the house to me in detail, room by room. Finally, she added that there was something else about this house. It had an indoor... swimming pool. That knocked me off my feet. Did God have his fingers in this? I replied that I would come to Szczecin for a weekend and we would see everything together. That is how it happened. We considered

Chapter 9 Bible – the instruction manual to life

all the pros and cons, and... decided to buy the house. In this way, one day in the future, I was to live in a house with a swimming pool.

Almost simultaneously, I received another signal from the Holy Spirit concerning my future. For some time we practiced in our 'Koinonia John the Baptist' community in Hamburg the daily morning prayer before starting work. At dawn, whoever could, would come to pray together. During one of these morning meetings a very clear and very strong message came to me. It was not some audible voice that spoke. No one but me heard it, but to me it was so very real, so real, and so emphatic that I was convinced it was the voice of God speaking to me. It took a second. One moment. While I was thinking about something else entirely, the thought popped into my head, 'Pack your bags!' It was so powerful, so surprising, so loud, and yet so uplifting, so warm and so tender, that I cried. To this day, though many years have passed, I remember the place where I stood at that moment. I remember who was standing on my right hand and who was standing on my left hand. Such a powerful experience! An experience that, under the circumstances, I could not handle.

I never thought about leaving Hamburg. I had good conditions here, I had a good job, friends, and a wonderful community of which I was the moderator. After all, I could not just drop everything overnight and leave. I didn't yet know what God had planned for me, but the short message 'Pack your bags!' was already working in me.

It is only in retrospect that I see how beautifully God has arranged everything. Several more years had to pass from the moment I heard 'Pack your bags!' to my actual return to Poland, but from that moment on, everything was subordinate to my leaving Hamburg, even though I had no idea what it was all about.

First the house with the swimming pool, and my apartment in it. I had to do something about it. Slowly, I began to think about how to furnish the place where I would live in the future. Although my future was tied to my approaching retirement age, I already had to take care of some home items, if only for the time of my short visits. My niece's husband painted the walls, I bought a lamps and some cabinets at a used furniture store. Someone gave me a couch and a bed for my bedroom. Slowly my apartment went equipped and ready for relocation. Only I was missing.

On the other hand, the company in which I had worked for fourteen years had financial problems and after unsuccessful attempts to save it, went bankrupt. I was left without a job. For a year I searched intensively for stable employment, and finally I took a temporary job in a rent-an-employee agency. For nine months I had to travel 90 kilometers to and from work for pitiful wages, working from morning to night. With such a physical burden, I was unable to adequately address the spiritual realm of my life. I resigned from the position of the community coordinator. I asked my superiors to transfer the responsibility of leading the community to another person.

In 2005, at the age of 54, I didn't have a permanent job, and in the community I descended to the position of an ordinary member. You could say – degradation in the material and spiritual areas. Although I managed to get a slightly better job in my profession, but it was a strictly temporary job, until the end of 2005. What would happen to me next? I didn't know. But God did know!

I was aware that at my age, I had no chance of finding a job in Hamburg. I did not want to spend the rest of my

Chapter 9 Bible – the instruction manual to life

life on welfare. I thought more and more about returning to my country. God arranged it all so that in this very difficult time for me the shepherd general and founder of 'Koinonia John the Baptist', Father Ricardo, came to our community in Hamburg. I asked him for conversation and direction. Father Ricardo, after he got to know my situation and heard that I would like to return to Poland, suggested that I go to the community in Gdynia. He also wanted to send Father Jan Kruczyński there. In this way I was to become Fr. Jan's assistant in evangelization and building 'Koinonia John the Babtist' in Gdynia. A dream situation for me, but also a great challenge.

'What if this plan fails? Something will go wrong? Something will fail? What about me then?' I knew only one thing. If I wanted to go back to Poland, I had to close everything in Hamburg. Burn the bridges. I did not know what would happen. But I felt that God requires this step from me and He is with me. That was enough for me. I began to prepare to leave Germany. I closed all the official matters. I released my apartment, closed my bank account. I was at the disposal of God and Father Jan, who was already in Gdynia, waiting for my arrival. On December 23, 2005 I went to work for the last time. I said goodbye to my colleagues. During the Christmas I said goodbye to my friends from the community. I had to answer questions that were very difficult for me at the time, 'What will you do next?', 'Where are you going?', 'What will you do for a living?' Each time the honest answer, 'I don't know!' I desperately wanted to avoid such questions. Unfortunately, everyone asked them. They were shaking their heads. And I didn't know what would happen to me next! I had a place to live in Szczecin, but God, who gave me 'a house with a swimming pool', told me to bypass that house and go to Gdynia, 450 kilometers away. I didn't even know where I would live there! All I had was Father Jan's phone number. That was all my insurance! I agreed with the priest that we would meet in Szczecin and then go to Gdynia, my new place of residence.

A joyful return

> *Like a hunted gazelle,*
> *or a flock that no one gathers,*
> *They shall turn each to their own people*
> *and flee each to their own land.*

Isaiah 13:14

In January 2006, after twenty years abroad, I left Germany and returned to Poland. I spent the first nine months with Father Jan. After five months we were joined by Agnieszka Zuzia Zuzelska, who was responsible for our office. Father Jan was responsible for building up the community, while Zuzia and I were entrusted with organizing and conducting meetings and evangelization courses – mainly in the field. In such conditions I was being born to live in a new, unfamiliar Polish reality. During that period God was constantly shaping a new character in me and taught me to be entirely dependent on Him.

It didn't matter that a nice two-room attic apartment in Hamburg was exchanged for a small room in Gdynia, where it was impossible to take three full steps. It didn't matter that I slept on a mattress sixty centimeters wide. The important thing was that I felt immersed in the embrace of the loving Father.

Father Jan, seeing Zuzia's evangelizing abilities, sent her to an evangelization school in Pilsen, in the Czech Republic.

Chapter 9 Bible – the instruction manual to life

Founded on the initiative of our community 'Koinonia John the Babtist', the school was to prepare people for world-wide missionary evangelization. Zuzia left for Czechia and, soon after her departure, Father Jan left for a community in Italy. I was to decide for myself.

During those nine months, surrounded by Father Jan's care, with the good advice that Zuzia gave me about life in Poland and with the support of the community, I felt very safe. When it came to me that I had to leave this place and start taking care of myself, I reacted by crying like a baby leaving her mother's womb.

How many tears I have shed since meeting God! There have been tears of joy, tears of sorrow, and tears of helplessness. And yet I was once told that a real man never cries. Good thing I found a remarkable passage in the Bible that talks about tears: *'My wanderings you have noted; are my tears not stored in your flask, recorded in your book?'*[14] These words made me feel secure. And even though I cried, I was a real man in God's eyes.

Leaving Gdynia, I could only take one direction – Szczecin and the house that was waiting for me, with the swimming pool, which was no longer there. My sister and her husband decided to demolish the pool and build a garden in its place. The time had come when I was supposed to live for good in the apartment prepared for my return.

It was not so bad, I had a roof over my head. But even with a roof over my head I would die of hunger. I had no means to live. Until then, Father Jan and I had benefited from the generosity of our community. But what now, when Father Jan is no longer here, and I live in Szczecin? I couldn't be a burden for my sister! I put everything on one card. 'Either

---
[14] Psalm 56:9

God will help me, or...?' I decided to fast until the time when I would know what to do next. On the third day of my strict fasting and prayer, a friend from the Baptist Church called me. He found out that I was in Szczecin and decided to invite me to a meeting with homeless and addicted people that he was organizing. There were going to be some people from England at the meeting who are there to help lost people. I wasn't feeling well either physically or spiritually and didn't want to leave the house. I just asked to be told where and at what time the meeting would be held, and I would surround them with my prayers.

Hours passed by. I prayed for the meeting, and the closer the meeting time got, the more I felt I had to be there! Finally, I decided that I would go. I showered and shaved and hit the road. During the meeting, the English guests spoke about how they try to help addiction-enslaved people in their country. Then there was a long prayer for divine intervention and finally a little refreshment. After the meeting, as I was about to leave the room, one of the Englishmen appeared in front of me with an interpreter. I understood that he probably wanted to tell me something. He reached into his jacket pocket, pulled out an envelope, and through the interpreter told me that God had told him to give this to me. I stood stunned for a moment with the envelope in my hand while the Englishman and the translator disappeared. I returned home and, telling my sister and brother-in-law what had happened to me, I opened the envelope. Inside was 5030 zlotys![15] It was another sign that God watches over me, listens to my requests and does not leave me without help in a difficult situation!

---

[15] About US$1,200

Chapter 9 Bible – the instruction manual to life

I already had a roof over my head, some cash to support myself, all I needed was a job. Where to find it? After twenty years of absence, Poland was an alien country for me and I could not move freely. I did not know how or where to look for employment, and I knew I needed a job.

Again, the words of the Bible came to my aid: *'What your hands provide you will enjoy; you will be blessed and prosper:'*[16] These words are a promise from God that He cannot renounce! In prayer, I began to remind God of this promise (as if He had forgotten!), 'God, do something! My finances are melting!' And then my brother-in-law brought me a newspaper with an ad saying that a 'Mabo Company' is looking for welders. I put down the address with the idea that I would find out where it was and visit the plant. Two days later I went to a shopping center. Returning home I saw the information by the side of the road: 'Mabo – 300 meters'. I followed the direction and after just a few moments I spoke to the manager of the welding section. I explained that I had recently returned from Germany and my work certificates were in German, but the manager was not interested. He just asked if I had experience as a welder and if I could start work tomorrow. He surprised me a little with this haste. We agreed that I would start work in the first days of November. That is how it happened. The amazing thing is that 5030 zlotys melted down to zero on the day of my first paycheck! Once again God has shown me that He is the driver. In this way, my confidence grew more and more.

The beginning of my work in Poland was not easy. I did not know the working conditions in my new place of employment. I was only told that I would be working on piecework, but that the first days would be on a daily basis so that I

---
[16] Psalm 128:2

could get into production. No one notified me when I was to start working piecework. For about two weeks I did this and that, helped here and there. I didn't know that I was supposed to write down everything I did, because at the end of the month you have to fill out a job card. Once I took up piecework, I wrote everything down and it was obvious to me. But when I worked on a daily basis, I was convinced that my manager was watching over everything and that he knew what I did. Unfortunately, that was not the case. In a German company it was a norm that the foreman knew everything about what the employee was doing. Unfortunately, in Poland it was completely different. When I received my first pay slip – I froze.

My days were not counted because I had not documented them. I was treated as if I had not been at work at all. I was paid only for piecework. It was also based on a contract for work. Of course, I was bitter, but what could I do? I could only thank God that I had a job. To alleviate my bitterness I laughed a little, telling my colleagues that the first German came to Poland to work and deserved the smallest payment.

When I left that plant after five years, my wages were among the highest in my category. Praise the Lord! The work I did required great physical effort, and since it was on piecework basis, I could not spare myself if I wanted to earn money. This is how my elbow joint failed. After an examination by an orthopedist, it was diagnosed that I couldn't continue to work like that. I was referred to the Center for Occupational Medicine, where it was confirmed that I was unable to continue working. In Poland, I was not entitled to any sickness allowance. I couldn't work in my profession, nor did I have any chance of other employment. So I decided to return to Germany and wait for my retirement age there,

Chapter 9 Bible – the instruction manual to life

registered as a job seeker. But thanks to this I could work intensively for the glory of the Lord.

The Holy Spirit has once again shown His power in my life. While I was still in Hamburg I had another strong conviction about the future. I was certain that one day I would evangelize on television. Again, this was contrary to what I thought of myself, and was beyond both my abilities and my imagination. I would have never invented it myself. Nevertheless, shortly after my return to Germany, I received an offer to record episodes of 'Word for Sunday'[17] for the Polish national television channel TVP2.

Earlier, still as a welder, I had recorded one episode thanks to my acquaintance with the director, Julita Wołoszyńska. Now TVP2 offered me to record more episodes. In this way, what the Holy Spirit had told me was fulfilled again.

I had an obligation to inform the relevant unemployment office in Germany about each of my movements in the field of work. So I went to this office with a contract between me and the Polish national broadcaster. The lady who dealt with my files asked me what position I would be hired in. She knew well my education and long experience in the profession of a locksmith-welder. Everything was in my files that she had in front of her. When I told her that the contract stated 'Journalist', she looked up from her documents and stared at me in disbelief as if asking, 'How is it possible for a man with a two-year vocational training in prison to get a position as a journalist on a national television network?' To tell the truth, I am surprised at it myself! But God is still the God of the unpredictable.

---

[17] 'A weekly religious program that discusses passages from the Bible provided in the Liturgy of the Word during Sunday masses in the Roman Catholic Church' (vod.tvp.pl). The program is broadcast nationwide.

Chapter 10
Post Scriptum

> *Do you not know that the runners in the stadium all run in the race, but only one wins the prize? Run so as to win.*
>
> 1 Corinthians 9:24

I TRIED to briefly describe 63 years of my life. The first, slightly longer part is 38 years downhill. In these 38 years, I have not recorded any significant success. However, almost every day was full of failures. Today, when I look back in search of successes, I am terrified. What have I achieved during these 38 years? What good have I done? I only remember one success from that time, and it was only because I was looking for it.

My greatest achievement was completing a two-year vocational school while serving a sentence in prison. These conditions mobilized me so much that I finished school with a very good result.

Apart from this – nothing more. I have failed in every area of my life. Each of my days was a journey downhill. I was descending to ever lower levels of existence. At some point, I found myself at the very bottom. I couldn't fail more. The only thing left for me then was suicide. My role in this world was over. Apart from death, there was no other perspective. This seemed then the only sensible way of changing my situation. 'Maybe someone who finds my body will consider me a hero because I have done such a great deed? Maybe this is how I will gain recognition?'

Thank God I didn't succeed in that too. A couple of suicide attempts – and nothing! Was it even in this my inability to achieve my goal, or was it an intervention of a loving God? I will not risk an answer here, although I will share my thoughts.

I believe that God did not allow me to die prematurely, because of His love for me. I can already hear the accusations, like 'God is unfair, because he loves some and does not allow them to commit suicide, while He cares not about others who die in a tragic way!' My answer will be the words of the Holy Scriptures, *'Because God did not make death, nor does he rejoice in the destruction of the living.'*[1]

God loves every human being, good and bad. Man has control over his life. But God has power over whatever circumstances the man finds himself in. It was me who decided to hang myself on the rope. God could not forbid me to do it because I decided it in my free will, which I had received from Him. God could not deprive me of my freedom of choice. But God could act through circumstances in which I was immersed. He could have caused the rope to break. Without violating my will, the Lord of life could save me from imminent death. We go back to the starting point: God, for unknown reasons, chose me to live. I searched for a long time for explanations regarding God's choice and God's justice. Today I managed to grasp it, to some extent.

---

[1] Wisdom 1:13

Chapter 10 Post Scriptum

Yes, God has His chosen people. Many Bible verses say this. It may sound unfair, but if we delve into it we discover that God chooses all but not everyone becomes God's chosen. Finally, the choice is not God's, but the choice is ours. God gives signs through various circumstances. Through these circumstances, God wants to attract human attention. You may notice these signs or fail to notice them. If a man responds to a given sign from God, he becomes the chosen one. If not, he eliminates himself from the 'privileged' society of the chosen. This is what St. Paul teaches us in his letter to the Romans (1:19–22):

> *For what can be known about God is evident to them, because God made it evident to them. Ever since the creation of the world, his invisible attributes of eternal power and divinity have been able to be understood and perceived in what he has made. As a result, they have no excuse; for although they knew God they did not accord him glory as God or give him thanks. Instead, they became vain in their reasoning, and their senseless minds were darkened. While claiming to be wise, they became fools.*

No one can claim that God ignored him. It is man ignoring God! In this situation, God can do nothing except give another sign, to make himself known through another circumstance. And He is often rejected, again and again. Where a man would have given up, God does not give up. He wants salvation for everyone. This is Love! Hundreds, thousands of times, rejected, but He does not quit. He always gives signs and waits. Maybe this time. Or maybe this time. Can you understand God's patience?

God has been waiting for me patiently for 38 years. How many signs have been sent to me during this time? How many times did He protect me? Only He knows that. Today, being aware of this, I can only kneel and say, 'Thank you God! Thank you for your patience! Thank you for not quitting when everyone gave up on me! Thank you!'

What would have happened to me if it hadn't been for this weak Polish woman working in the soup kitchen for the homeless? For 38 years nobody was able to take care of me so effectively. At this point, I always remember the parable of the Good Samaritan. The man in this story was going down from Jerusalem to Jericho. Jerusalem is situated in the mountains of Judea. The Hebrew name of this city is *Yerushalaim*, which translates as 'City of Peace'. The man had just left that City of Peace on the mountain and was going down to another city, Jericho. Jericho is located approximately 270 meters below the sea level. It's like 'underground', a metaphor of the abyss, the biblical *Sheol*. As he descended, he fell victim of muggers who robbed him of everything he had. All he had was a remnant of his life. He was still alive, but was already on his way into the abyss, into the underground 'Jericho'. Why am I writing about this? Precisely to illustrate my thirty-eight years of existence.

At some point in my life, I left God and the City of Peace. I started my long journey downhill. I had no idea that without God it could only get worse, worse and worse. During this long descent, I was beaten, robbed, abused, wounded in a variety ways, and finally – abandoned half-dead. You could say that everyone passed me, walked away from me. All that was left for me was the abyss, the *Sheol*. Then I met my Good Samaritan. The woman I met in the soup kitchen was deeply moved by my situation and took care of my wounds. She brought me to the 'inn', which is the Church. There

Chapter 10 Post Scriptum

the wounds inflicted on me over the years could be healed and I was prepared for a new journey, this time up the hill, to heavenly Jerusalem. This is what conversion really is! 'Conversion' indeed means a change of direction. Before I was going down all the time. By turning to God, I changed my position, I started to climb.

With God, not only did I begin to recover what I had been brutally deprived of, but I also began to achieve what I would never have achieved on my own. Today I know who I am. I know what I am doing and why. Most importantly, I know where I am going. Towards the finish line. Towards the reward. To eternal happiness with Jesus Christ. For now, I stick to the signpost that my Lord has given me:

> *I am coming quickly. Hold fast to what you have, so that no one may take your crown.*
>
> *The victor I will make into a pillar in the temple of my God, and he will never leave it again. On him I will inscribe the name of my God and the name of the city of my God, the new Jerusalem, which comes down out of heaven from my God, as well as my new name.* (Revelation 3:11–12)

All of this is still ahead of me. In order to reach the goal, I must constantly remember that without my Lord and Savior I cannot achieve anything. I know my failures in the life without God. Now I see clearly the success to which my good, loving Father is leading me.

When I speak of the success, I do not mean wealth, material goods, career. Everything that most people strive for and recognize as success fades in comparison to what you can get from the Triune God. After all, you cannot buy inner peace or health for a million zlotys. Money can only be used to pay for medicines, not for health. You will not find patience or gentleness in a luxurious car.

St. Paul in his Letter to the Galatians (5) details what vain boasting is (i.e. success) and what is the value of the fruit of the Spirit. I think all people desire love, joy, peace, patience, kindness, generosity, faithfulness, gentleness, and self-control. A man who produces such fruit is a man of success! By discovering such abilities in yourself, you discover your value and dignity, which God gives to man for free.

Although everything we get from God is free, we still must fight to keep it. This is the cross that Jesus spoke about. Resist the old nature of sin and cultivate the fruit of the Spirit. I have already made up my mind. I will not give up! I know a great reward in heaven will await me if I persevere. If you, dear Reader, have not yet entrusted your life to the One who gave it to you, do so now, when you have read my story. God loves you and there has never been a day in your life when you were not loved! Even when you had a very hard time and you thought that everyone abandoned you – God never did!

I, too, once thought that I was left alone, but that was due to a misunderstanding of God's love. I thought that since God loves me, he should automatically activate some system to protect me. However, God loves me so much that He has given me free will. I am the one who decides whether God's love will reach me or not. When I turn my back on God and think that I will manage my life better, He cannot do anything!

This turning away from God is called sin. It does not have to be some explicit crime, such as theft or murder, for example. It is the invisible sin of mistrust against God. It is because I don't believe God wants the best for me. This sin was born in a garden called Eden when Adam and Eve

Chapter 10 Post Scriptum

doubted God's guidance and decided to take the matter into their own hands. Immediately after that, Adam hid from God.

Man born with the nature of the first Adam suffers the condition of hiding from God. Without knowing it – we run away from God's love! The relationship between the loving God and a person in need of love is broken. God knows that a man cannot repair this broken relationship on his own. God's law says, *'the wages of sin is death,'*[2] and it is only by the death of a person that such situations can be changed. Does God want man to die? By no means! God is a lover of life. What does God do in such a situation? He, in his love for man, becomes man. Jesus Christ came into the world. He assumed the body of a human being to die as a human being. He who committed no sin on the Cross took all the sins of mankind upon Himself! Why did he do it? For the love of man.

God's justice was accomplished through the death of Jesus the man – man sinned, man died because of sin. From the moment Jesus died on the cross, each person can enter into a relationship with the loving God. Jesus Christ is the connecting link between God and man.

Jesus Christ is the solution to all your problems. He, with his hand outstretched, is waiting for you. Do you want to give Him your hand? I did it 24 years ago and I have no doubt that Jesus is lifting me to the pinnacle of my life. Do you want it too? Maybe you're asking: 'how?' It's easy. Believe that God has something wonderful for you and turn away from mundane thinking and behavior like: 'I have to take care of everything myself.' Decide not to follow the pattern of the fallen world and start following God's

---

[2] Romans 6:23

instructions for life. In this way, you will be born again for God and your life will gain wind in its sails.

When you make up your mind, Jesus will send on you the Holy Spirit, who will lead you on the way that you have been looking for, but not yet found. The Holy Spirit, the third divine Person, from now on will be your strength, your guide, your protection. Then you and the author of the Psalm 91 will be able to recite:

> *You who dwell in the shelter of the Most High,*
> *who rest in the shade of the Almighty,*
>
> *Say to the Lord, 'My refuge and fortress,*
> *my God in whom I trust.'*
>
> *He will rescue you from the fowler's snare,*
> *from the destroying plague,*
>
> *He will shelter you with his pinions,*
> *and under his wings you may take refuge;*
> *his faithfulness is a protecting shield.*
>
> *You shall not fear the terror of the night*
> *nor the arrow that flies by day,*
>
> *Nor the pestilence that roams in darkness,*
> *nor the plague that ravages at noon.*
>
> *Though a thousand fall at your side,*
> *ten thousand at your right hand,*
> *near you it shall not come.*
>
> *You need simply watch;*
> *the punishment of the wicked you will see.*
>
> *Because you have the Lord for your refuge*
> *and have made the Most High your stronghold,*
>
> *No evil shall befall you,*
> *no affliction come near your tent.*

Chapter 10 Post Scriptum

For he commands his angels with regard to you,
to guard you wherever you go.

With their hands they shall support you,
lest you strike your foot against a stone.

You can tread upon the asp and the viper,
trample the lion and the dragon.

Because he clings to me I will deliver him;
because he knows my name I will set him on high.

He will call upon me and I will answer;
I will be with him in distress;
I will deliver him and give him honor.

With length of days I will satisfy him,
and fill him with my saving power.

How are you to receive Jesus Christ into your life? Like me and many of my friends have done. Through prayer! And if you don't know how to pray, I offer you the following formula:

Lord Jesus. I need you. I believe you are the Son of God. I believe you died on the cross for my sins. Now I am asking you to forgive me for all my transgressions. I welcome you now into my life as my only Lord and Savior. From now on, I am asking for your guidance in my life. I want to belong to you. You died for me, so now I am dying for my old way of life. I want to live a new life from you. Make me the way you want me. Amen!

Now that you have decided to connect to God's love, take one more step as soon as possible – join God's family. Please do not hesitate and find your place in the community of believers. Join the Church. If you are already in the Church, find a fellowship there in which you will be able to grow. Remember! Your presence in the Church once a week is a minimum. Find people who meet each week to pray and study God's Word. Only in this way will you grow into a great winner and leader.

This is the end of this book, but not the end of my life story. I have many years of abundant life with God ahead of me. In my experience, God always has something better for me tomorrow. Therefore, full of confidence, I look forward to what will happen in the future. Maybe a day will come when I begin to carry on with what I am finishing now. Maybe there will be another book. Everything is in the hands of God, whom I want to serve with all my strength and with all my heart.

Thank you, dear Reader, for choosing to devote some of your precious time to the story of my life. It is important that you do not overlook what I wanted to include in this book: the main character of this story is the loving God the Father, his Son, Jesus Christ, who gave me a new life and the Holy Spirit who guides me through this life. Without the Triune God, this book would never have been written, and I would certainly have said goodbye to life long ago.

Chapter 10 Post Scriptum

**To Him
who created all things
and sustains all things
by the power of His word,
be glory now
and forever!
Amen!**

Contents

1	Childhood and youth	7
2	Life and marriage	19
3	My nighttime shelters	43
4	God steps in	63
5	A new beginning	79
6	Growing in the spirit	95
7	Real signs	115
8	Return to family	131
9	Bible – the instruction manual to life	153
10	Post Scriptum	185

Printed in Poland
by Amazon Fulfillment
Poland Sp. z o.o., Wrocław

16127069R00112